The International Economy Since 1945

In *The International Economy Since 1945*, Sidney Pollard describes the most important global developments in economic affairs during the last half-century. This comprehensive history covers all geographical regions and looks at the effects of the major countries on each other.

The International Economy Since 1945 details worldwide issues as well as institutional issues. The author considers the impact of policies on economic life and includes discussion of

- the impact of World War II on global economy
- the threat to the environment caused by economic change
- advances in technology as they relate to growth
- fluctuations in standards of living in all parts of the globe
- policies, and how they influence growth
- reactions of other nations to the plight of the Third World
- the communist and Far Eastern economies

Sidney Pollard explores the relationships between the recent stagnation and decline in most economies and economic policies. *The International Economy Since 1945* debates the key issues of current global and national policy making and the effects of greater economic integration on inflation and employment.

Sidney Pollard is Senior Honorary Fellow of the University of Sheffield.

The Making of the Contemporary World
Edited by Eric Evans and Ruth Henig
University of Lancaster

The Making of the Contemporary World series provides challenging interpretations of contemporary issues and debates within strongly defined historical frameworks. The range of the series is global, with each volume drawing together material from a range of disciplines – including economics, politics and sociology. The books in this series present compact, indispensable introductions for students studying the modern world.

Forthcoming titles include:

The International Economy Since 1945

Sidney Pollard

London and New York

First published 1997
by Routledge
11 New Fetter Lane, London EC4P 4EE

Simultaneously published in the USA and Canada
by Routledge
29 West 35th Street, New York, NY 10001

© 1997 Sidney Pollard

Phototypeset in Times by Intype London Ltd
Printed and bound in Great Britain by Mackays of Chatham PLC,
Chatham, Kent

British Library Cataloguing in Publication Data
A catalogue record for this book is available from the British Library

Library of Congress Cataloguing in Publication Data
A catalogue record for this book has been requested
ISBN 0–415–14067–6

Contents

Illustrations

1 Introduction
The world economy after the war, 1945–50

EFFECTS OF THE WAR

The Second World War which came to an end in 1945 had caused more destruction, human as well as material, than any previous conflict. Europe had suffered most, together with Japan, but there was massive destruction also in China and south-eastern Asia, there had been much fighting which ravaged North Africa, and all maritime nations had sustained grievous losses at sea. The United States, Canada, Australia and New Zealand, among others, had devoted enormous resources to the war though they had been spared actual warfare on their territory, and, together with the colonial dependencies of the European powers, they mourned many killed and injured in the forces. Few areas of the globe outside Latin America were left unaffected.

In Europe alone, between 40 and 45 million people lost their lives: no exact count is possible, since many of those who died, especially among the more than 20 million victims in the Soviet Union, were civilians who perished in air raids, in labour camps or on the road, having been driven out of their homes. About 6 million Jews were killed in the Nazi death camps. Three million non-Jewish Poles and 1.6 million Yugoslavs also lost their lives. When the fighting ended, there were some 15 million 'displaced persons' awaiting repatriation. To these have to be added the missing births, and the millions of the injured.

China's military losses included 1.3 million dead, while an additional 9 million civilians died in the war period and a further 4 million in the famine of 1945–6. Japan lost 2.5 million dead, and the human losses among other Asian countries, mostly civilian, may have numbered up to 5 million. American losses among the armed forces totalled 400,000 dead and 700,000 wounded, and other Allied non-European losses among fighting men and civilians added a further 2.5 million dead. The total may well have exceeded 60 million people who died as a result of the war.

The psychological costs of all these human disasters are incalculable, as are the traumatic effects of the nuclear bombs on Hiroshima and Nagasaki on the survivors. Not least, there was a residue of national hatred which poisoned many parts of the world for years to come.

Among material losses, damage to housing and other buildings loomed large. In the Soviet Union 17,000 towns and 70,000 villages were destroyed, while Germany lost 20 per cent of her housing stock and Britain 9 per cent in the bombing, as well as damage to many more. Capital was run down or wrecked all over Europe: factories had been bombed, railway tracks destroyed, bridges were down. Thus the Soviet Union had 65,000 km of railway track and 13,000 bridges destroyed. Of the 17,000 pre-war French locomotives, only 3,000 were serviceable. Despite much building, both the British and Japanese mercantile fleets were 4½ million gross tons down on pre-war, Germany's shipping was reduced from 4½ million to 700,00 gross tons, and Italy's from 3.4 million to 700,000 gross tons. Many harbours were blocked and canals had been put out of action. Agriculture also suffered grievously: in Poland, for example, it was estimated that 60 per cent of farm livestock had been lost.

The destruction affected different parts of the world most unevenly. Worst hit were Germany, eastern Europe, large areas of China, and Japan, but there was much damage also in western Europe including Britain, in Italy and in Greece. In the areas most affected, the outlook seemed grim indeed. Factories needed fuel and raw materials to restart, but these could not be delivered because the means of transport were out of action, and these could not be repaired because the factories were not working. Agricultural output was down because so many of the men had been killed, as well as because of the lack of equipment and fertilizer, and as a result workers in towns were undernourished and less productive. The breakdown of normal economic relations was marked in some countries by the replacement of money by barter exchange, or the use of cigarettes as currency. Much labour had to be devoted just to clear the rubble and provide temporary housing. In many areas the economic problems seemed insoluble, and relief agencies, such as the United Nations Relief and Rehabilitation Administration (UNRRA), had to devote much of their resources simply to ensure bare survival.

As the conflict of 1939–45 had fully engaged the economies of the industrialized belligerents especially in Europe and Japan, their traditional role of supplying manufactures to the rest of the world had largely fallen into abeyance in the war years. The United States had still much surplus capacity and filled some of the gaps, particularly in Latin America, but other economies had to look to their own resources to meet their demand for manufactures, and there was a considerable indigenous growth of industry in such countries and regions as Australia, South Africa, South America and parts of Asia. Much of this industry would be vulnerable to competition from the advanced world, once peace conditions returned, but some survived as the basis for successful post-war industrialization.

The traditional exports of the non-European world, consisting of raw materials and food products, were also in high demand, which was possibly even strengthened in the early peace years, as in so many areas simply to have enough food for sheer survival had overriding priority. It was also the case that at the time it was more difficult to raise the productivity on farms than in factories. In fact, the output of most foodstuffs, apart from rice, which was not a major food grain in the western world, stagnated in the war years, while world population increased. World wheat production actually fell from 176 million tons in 1938 to 157 million tons in 1948. European grain and potato crops had in 1947 fallen to two-thirds of their pre-war level. The result was that the prices of 'primary products' rose faster than the prices of manufactured products, and the tendency was reinforced by the stockpiling of raw materials in the Korean war boom of 1951–2. The relative prices between these two types of commodities, manufactures and primary products, known as the 'terms of trade', thus turned at least for a time in favour of countries exporting the latter, mainly food and raw materials, which mostly meant the poorer countries outside Europe.

The countries not directly occupied or damaged tended to be relative gainers from the changes produced by the war. This was above all true of the United States. As far as manufactures were concerned, the USA produced almost half the world's total in 1946, compared with only 32 per cent in 1936–8, while containing only 6 per cent of world population. Her mercantile marine rose from 17 per cent of the world's tonnage in 1939 to 53 per cent in 1947. Latin America, too, was a gainer: its share of world exports rose from 7–8 per cent in 1938 to 13–14 per cent in 1946, though much of that trade was among the region's countries themselves. It was symbolic for the region's progress that its energy consumption had risen by 82 per cent between 1939 and 1947. In Africa, the regions supplying important materials, such as the Belgian Congo, East Africa and South Africa, gained: the rest actually lost out. Europe, which had accounted for 47 per cent of world trade in 1938, had seen its share shrink to 41 per cent in 1948.

Yet recovery, at least among the industrialized belligerent nations, was remarkably rapid. There were many reasons for that resilience. For one thing, while much civilian production had been stopped in the war years, there was substantial new engineering, metalworking and chemical capacity created for armaments production, much of which could easily be converted to peacetime uses. Moreover, the infrastructure, such as roads, bridges or power lines, was in place, and, though badly damaged, had merely to be repaired. Above all, there were skilled and knowledgeable people, workers and technicians, used to industrial and social discipline, who could be mobilized fairly quickly to set the wheels going again. There was also a long tradition of saving and capital creation, of reasonably competent government and effective markets. Additionally, help came in the form of machines, raw materials and food from the undamaged countries such as the USA and Canada, some of it, as we shall see later, provided free or against long-term repayment.

MEASUREMENT OF NATIONAL INCOME

Thus by 1950 the available statistical information shows that most affected countries had reached income levels well above those of pre-war, and others were rapidly approaching these. The composition of the goods and services they consumed might be different, but in total, what is known as the 'Gross National Product' (GNP) per head showed a clear advance over the 1930s. This concept of GNP will appear again later, and it will therefore be worthwhile to explain briefly what is meant by it, its usefulness and its dangers.

The idea behind the GNP is to add together all goods and services made available within the economy; if we divide that total by the number of people, we get GNP per head. Double counting has to be avoided: thus we do not count the output of steel *and* the output of cars into which it enters, but only the latter. If we deduct all goods and services which go into replacing capital worn out, on the grounds that this does not really represent anything available to people as consumers and is really a cost, we arrive at Net National Product (NNP). Armed with such figures, we can then proceed to

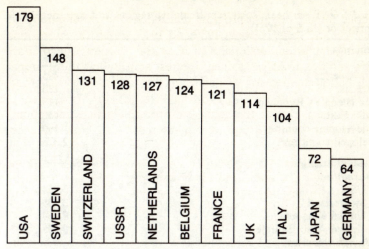

Figure 1.1 GNP at constant prices in 1950 in selected countries, 1938 = 100

compare the totals of goods and services available in different years for one country, or in different countries, provided we value everything at the same 'constant' prices. Thus we can see whether output and standards of living have been growing or declining, and how one country or region compares with another.

Such calculations are not without their problems. Thus it is difficult for the statisticians to count the foodstuffs consumed on farms themselves which do not enter any markets; or, to cite another example, we do not count the work of housewives in the home. If they bake their own bread, their contribution is not counted; but if they buy from the baker, it does become part of the registered 'national product': this means that the figures will show an increase in output where none had occurred. These and other gaps affect low-income countries far more than richer nations, and GNP or NNP figures are therefore particularly suspect when comparisons are made between these two types of economies. Thus if we see GNP figures which show, say, American incomes to be fifty times higher than incomes in some parts of the Third World, such figures should not be taken as precise meaningful measurements, but merely as general indications. Among similar economies, however, the GNP and NNP measures are the best means available to compare relative production totals and rates of change.

Figure 1.1 shows that the United States which had worked at far below full employment in the 1930s and therefore started out with

Table 1.1 GNP per head: some representative regions and countries, 1950 (in prices of US $ of 1974)

South Asia	85
Africa	170
Latin America	495
East Asia	130
China (People's Republic)	113
Middle East	460
All developing countries	160
Developed countries*	2,378
Individual examples:	
Rich countries	
USA	3,954
Switzerland	3,938
United Kingdom	2,064
United Arab Emirates	9,635
Fairly rich countries	
Italy	1,409
Argentina	907
Very poor countries	
Philippines	168
India	95
Ethiopia	58

* All OECD except Greece, Portugal, Spain, Turkey
Source: Based on World Bank statistics

much spare capacity, had registered the most impressive growth. The neutrals in the war, Sweden and Switzerland, had also improved their position by wide margins. But even among the belligerents, the victors stood well above their pre-war levels. Among the Axis losers, Italy had recovered more successfully than Germany or Japan.

However, the really large differences were still those between different parts of the world. The position as it appeared in 1950, when the worst of the war damage had been made good in the west, is illustrated in Table 1.1.

Even if we bear in mind the remarks made above on the problems of assigning GNP figures to poor economies and take account of differences of climate, social structure and tradition, it is clear that the poverty of non-European countries was of a different order from the temporary problems of the European nations. The scourge of disease and the high death rates, the widespread hunger and the lack of amenities prevalent in many of those areas, were of a kind unimaginable to Europeans. Nevertheless, possibly because the plight of the non-Europeans was of long standing, while Europe had suffered a drastic deterioration, and possibly also because it had more political clout and believed that its ills could more easily be remedied, it was the latter which received the greater attention at the time.

THE ROLE OF THE USA IN THE WORLD ECONOMY

The Europeans, suffering what to them were unparalleled shortages of food, of fuel, raw materials and capital equipment in the immediate post-war years, saw the only possible source of supply to lie in the surplus stocks and the undamaged productive powers of North America – if only these could be afforded. But to pay for them required dollars: far more dollars than the rest of the world possessed or could get hold of.

In consequence, in the post-war years the economic outlook of the industrialized world came to be dominated by the so-called 'dollar shortage'. At the time, it seemed to symbolize a fundamental and permanent shift, as a result of the war, in the distribution of the world's economic weight, away from Europe and towards North America. It looked as though it would never be possible to catch up on the productivity of the USA, since that country not only had the richer natural resources, but also, being richer, could invest more capital year by year, and thus always keep ahead technologically. As it turned out, this fear was misplaced, and the dollar shortage was to be short-lived, but this remained hidden from contemporaries. We shall see below how it was overcome in due course, but even after the dollar had ceased to be scarce, the dominant role of the United States remained and was to become a permanent feature of the world economy for the next half-century and beyond.

POLITICAL CHANGES

Such economic hegemony as the USA enjoyed could not be divorced from political power. Unlike the period following the First World War, when the United States had similarly entered the fighting at a late stage, to make a decisive contribution to victory for the Allies, but had then withdrawn into isolationism, this time she determined to take her place as the leading political power. Backed by her overwhelming economic as well as military might, she became one of the two 'superpowers' in the second half of the twentieth century, the other being the Soviet Union. For that and other reasons, the history of the world economy in that period cannot in fact be separated from the political developments which formed the framework within which the world economy had to operate.

Three political changes which followed the end of the Second World War stand out in importance in this context. The first of these was the division of the industrialized world into two hostile camps: the western, 'capitalist' and largely democratic countries, led by the United States as the dominant power, and the eastern, 'socialist' countries, dominated by the Soviet Union. From being allies in the war, the two superpowers and their satellites or supporters eyed each other with increasing suspicion from 1947 onwards. The Soviet Union expanded westward, absorbing the three Baltic states and parts of Poland, Germany and Romania; she also used the power of the Red Army to help to install communist governments in a number of her eastern European neighbours. The United States, for her part, used her economic power to prevent countries in the rest of the world from following the same path, and surrounded the Soviet Union with a ring of threatening military bases. Each of them tied their allies to themselves by tight military alliances, NATO and the Warsaw Pact, respectively.

Though armed to the teeth with increasingly costly, sophisticated and lethal nuclear weapons and means of delivering them, they avoided going to war with each other directly, merely keeping going a state of hostility which became known as the 'Cold War'. However, several proxy armed conflicts were fought, the most destructive of them being the Korean war (1950–3), the Vietnam conflict (1965–75) which involved the USA in a major way, and the Afghanistan war (1979–88) in which the USSR got embroiled. Additionally, there were numerous minor conflicts, including several bitter civil wars. The confrontation between east and west dominated world politics, diplomacy and military affairs in those years, and, as we shall see, was bound to affect economic development also. China, much the most populous country in the world, was at first part of the communist camp, but later took an independent line, though still adhering to a Marxist–socialist philosophy. She continued on this path even after the collapse of communist rule in the Soviet Union and her allies in 1989. Countries in neither orbit and not directly involved in that confrontation, mainly the less developed economies, became known as the 'Third World'.

The second main development in the political field was de-colonization. While the loser countries, as was traditional, had to give up some territory, and Japan and Italy lost their colonies, this time the victors also ceded some of their 'possessions', by giving independence to their overseas colonies in a long-drawn-out process after the end of the war. The countries mainly affected were Britain, France, the Netherlands, Belgium and the United States. In the 1970s their example was followed by Portugal. The complex process of handing over power to indigenous governments was carried through peacefully in many cases; in others it was accompanied by armed conflict. This was particularly so where a large European minority, belonging to the former colonial power, refused to give up without a fight, as in (French) Algeria, where fighting went on from 1954 to 1962 or in (British) Southern Rhodesia, later renamed Zimbabwe, between its illegal declaration of independence in 1965 and 1979.

The process created a large number of formally independent countries which came to dominate, at least numerically, such international bodies as the United Nations (of which more below). However, although their voices have in consequence not been entirely ineffective, most of them were poor, their economy was often unbalanced, and they lacked the skilled manpower and the political traditions which might have enabled them to catch up quickly in the economic field on the advanced world. Many of them remained dependent on the industrialized countries, which usually meant their former colonial power. In the case of the United Kingdom, they remained members of a restructured 'Commonwealth'. In return, they were given preference in the allocation of aid, and were granted special privileges by the European Community in the so-called Yaoundé and Lomé conventions, to be noted below.

The third major political innovation was the creation of a number of international bodies and conventions. The most comprehensive of these organizations was the United Nations (UN), which was intended to include every country in the world: from its original membership of 51 it has grown to the current (1996) membership of 185. Formally, it may be considered to be the successor of the League of Nations, founded after the First World War. But the victor countries of the Second World War who shaped its constitution sought to avoid the mistakes of the inter-war years, and while pursuing the same aim of avoiding wars and creating conditions for the peaceful co-existence of states, they gave it the means of more effective control of events, not least by creating the Security Council which has the strongest countries as permanent members. It was recognized from the beginning that the UN would not be able to stop wars among the major powers, but, as it turned out, it has not been able to stop minor wars either, and its efforts to secure, or enforce, the peace in various parts of the world has not been conspicuously successful.

Nevertheless, it created a framework of international discussion and agreement, and it has contributed something towards reducing, or punishing, the kind of political lawlessness which so disfigured the inter-war years: where it failed, it was either because a major power bloc vetoed its action, or because it was hamstrung by the convention that it could not interfere in the internal affairs of its member states. Its agencies, such as the United Nations Educational, Scientific and Cultural Organization (UNESCO), the Economic and Social Council which set in train numerous reports in its field, the International Court of Justice, and the Food and Agriculture Organization (FAO), among others, have not only made excellent contributions, particularly to the life of the poorer countries, but have strengthened the framework of collaboration, mutual aid and understanding for which the UN agencies were formed. Despite all the criticism which has been levied at them, the work of the UN agencies greatly exceeds anything of that nature ever attempted in human history before.

The rest of this book is divided into two parts: Part I (Chapters 2 to 5) will deal with economic developments in general, and Part II (Chapters 6 to 8) will deal with some problems arising from these developments and the policies devised to deal with them.

Part I
Economic development

2 Production and productivity

GROWTH IN OUTPUT AND PRODUCTIVITY

The world saw many economic changes between the 1940s and the 1990s. It is not too much to say that anyone who had gone to sleep in the post-war years and woken up again in the last years of the century, would have been faced by so many innovations that they would hardly recognize the environment they once knew. Certainly, no other period of history of equal length could compare with the developments of that half-century on a world scale.

Underlying this transformation was an unprecedented increase in production and productivity. This played a key role, perhaps *the* key role in the economic history of the world. There is a real sense in which it both determined the nature of these changes, and was the most tangible symbol of them.

Ideally, we should be able to represent that growth in figures. As we saw in Chapter 1, the accuracy of GNP calculations leaves something to be desired; nevertheless, they form the best approximation to a picture of overall growth that we possess, and some important data based on them are presented in Table 2.1.

In this table, the period 1950–94 has been divided into two parts, the dividing line being the year 1975. There are some differences between the two halves of the table, introduced to show that it is possible to vary the statistical representation. The GNP of the years 1950–75 is replaced by GDP (Gross Domestic Product) for the later years: this excludes the effects of imports and exports, which normally more or less balance, so that there is usually very little difference between these two measures. More significantly, the earlier years show growth per head, the later show total growth. Where, as in most of the Third World, there was a rapid population increase, in some cases exceeding 1 per cent per annum, the per

Table 2.1 Changes in GNP and GDP, major regions, in constant prices, 1950–1994

	GNP per capita Increase 1950–75, %		GDP Increase 1975–94, %		
	Total	Annual	Total	Annual	
South Asia	55	1.7 ⎫			
East Asia	162	3.9 ⎬	255	6.5	Asia
China	183	4.2 ⎭			
Africa	81	2.4	53	2.3	Africa*
Middle East	261	5.2	68	2.8	Middle East*
Latin America	91	2.6	70	2.7	Western hemisphere
All developing countries	134	3.4	115	4.1	Developing countries*
Developed countries	120	3.2	65	2.5	Industrial countries
			79	3.1	World*

* To 1993
Source: Based on World Bank and IMF statistics

capita growth will have been much slower than the increase of total production, because that now has to be shared among more people. These differences have to be watched when reading statistics of this kind. The advantage of considering total growth, particularly when the population is expanding, is that it shows the efforts which the economy has had to make to provide both for growth *and* for the additional population. Against this, per capita figures are a better indicator of productivity changes.

The table shows one way of dividing up the world total into categories of countries, but it is possible to group them in different ways. We might, for example, order them by levels of income. Thus the World Bank data allow us to learn that in the period 1950–75, GDP per capita grew by 1.1 per cent a year in lower-income countries, by 3.7 per cent in middle-income countries, by 3.4 per cent in upper- to middle-income countries and by 5.2 per cent in higher-income countries. Kuznets has shown how countries within each of the income groups are distributed among the geographical divisions, and Rostow has attempted to use the per capita income level in order to determine the stage of economic progress reached by each country.[1]

These groups are not homogeneous. The growth rates of individual countries within each group may vary widely, none more so than Russia and the other former communist states in their first years of 'liberalization', compared with the other countries among the middle-income economies. According to the World Bank, their per capita income *fell* by –1.7 per cent in 1990, by –8.5 per cent in 1991 and by a drastic –14.0 per cent in 1992, while the remainder of the countries in that group showed quite healthy positive growth rates. At the other end of the spectrum, the members of the European Common Market enjoyed growth rates of 5–6 per cent p.a. over long periods in the 1950s and 1960s, Japan had growth rates as high as 9–10 per cent p.a., while Korea, Singapore, Taiwan and Hong Kong, the 'Eastern tigers', exceeded even those rates for years on end.

These last may be considered exceptional cases, or exceptional periods. But even for the more humdrum results of the advanced world as a whole, which included some slow growers, the table shows an increase of GNP by two and a quarter times to 1975, having already registered fast growth to 1950; it increased by more than half again to the mid-1990s. Most of the less advanced areas grew faster still. In one way, these results may be taken as an impressive example of the power of compound interest, if continued for any length of time. Thus a growth of 2 per cent per annum over fifty years, will increase the total by some 2.7 times; 3 per cent per annum over 100 years would mean a growth to more than *nineteen* times the original figure.

These rates of growth after the end of World War II, for such a large number of countries and over so long a period, are unparalleled in history. Even in the nineteenth century which is often considered to have been a phase of rapid growth, world industrial production had seen growth of less than 3.5 per cent per annum, while in 1948–71 it was growing at a rate of 5.6 per cent. As for GDP as a whole, in the sixteen advanced countries studied by Maddison for which data exist, the average rate of real growth per capita had been:

1.4 per cent in 1870–1913;
1.2 per cent in 1913–50; but
3.8 per cent in 1950–73,

though it slowed down thereafter, following the first oil crisis of that year. This remarkable growth was achieved while hours of work were actually reduced, so that productivity, if measured by real GDP increase per man-hour, rose by no less than 4.5 per cent per annum in 1950–73, and even kept up a growth rate of 2.7 per cent in the depression years 1973–9, in those sixteen countries.[2]

THE SOURCES OF GROWTH

How were these high rates of productivity and output increases achieved? Economists tend to divide the sources of growth into two groups: one consists of increased inputs, mainly of capital and labour, since land, the third factor of production, can rarely be increased; the other contains all other causes, called 'residuals', though this should not be taken to imply that they are unimportant.

Increased labour input, which in this case means more people at work, has certainly been an important feature of the past half-century. Outside the industrialized countries, there has been a sharp increase of population as well as a larger proportion of them working for the market; in the advanced world, there has been an increase in the participation of women in paid work, though there has at the same time been a great expansion of the number of young people in full-time and part-time education, removing them from the work force. The larger proportion of older people has been approximately matched by the falling number of children, so that there was little change of the share of the population of working age. However, the rapidly rising per capita output, and even more significantly, output per man-hour, mean that we must look for causes other than an increase in the supply of labour.

The quantity of capital used in the production process has also been augmented in those years. In the industrialized countries capital input has gone up roughly in line with output, fluctuating around a steady 20–22 per cent of GNP year by year, though the rates for individual countries diverged widely from this norm. Since GNP itself was rising, this means that the sums set aside for investment were increasing in concrete terms. The developing countries did better still, since even the proportion invested was actually increasing substantially over our period, from an average of 16–18 per cent until 1972, to an average of 22–25 per cent thereafter. Much of this increase in that group of countries was due to the high rates of investment achieved by countries in the Far East and among the oil producers of the Middle East.

Increased capital investment has undoubtedly been an important source of growth. There are, however, some problems with these calculations. Given the technical progress of the age, a machine of 1995, costing perhaps the same as one doing similar work in 1950, will be far more efficient and productive: its quality will have gone up. At the same time, since the efficiency or productivity of the engineering industry which produced that machine will also have gone up, it will have cost less in real terms than its equivalent in 1950. The impact of the capital input on the growth in production is therefore likely to be greater than would be indicated by the rise in the sums spent on investment.

The 'residuals' are made up of several components. One important source of growth is the switch of resources, especially of labour, from activities of lower to those of higher productivity. Thus if, typically in the course of national economic development, men or women move out of agriculture, where their output is low, into industry, where they create greater values, national output will go up even if there is no change in the efficiency of either agriculture or industry as such. Such transfers did actually occur on a large scale all over the world in our period, and they form a main component of the structural change which has been a feature everywhere of economic growth. 'Traditional' economies, in Europe in the eighteenth century, or in parts of Africa and South Asia into our day, have up to 90 per cent of their population working on the land. With economic development, the share of manufacturing, mining and transport, known as the 'secondary' sector, rises at the expense of agriculture: its peak is usually reached when it accounts for a share of 40–45 per cent of employment, after which it declines. At that point, employment in the services, the so-called 'tertiary' sector, begins to increase until, in the most advanced countries, it tops 50 per cent of total employment, the labour force in agriculture having meanwhile shrunk to less than 10 per cent, its share of production being smaller still. Some data for the male labour force in a number of representative European countries are assembled in Table 2.2. In those six countries alone, male agricultural employment fell in thirty years from 15 million to 4 million, or by almost three-quarters, while men in services increased from 19 millions to 28 millions, or by almost one-half. The proportions of females active in the tertiary sector were higher still. A similar movement from lower to higher productive jobs went on *within* the three main sectors.

It is worth noting that the structural changes in employment with which growth is invariably associated also bring profound social changes in their wake. The life of a family moving from working on the land into an industrial employment in a town, or, to take another example, changing from 'blue-collar' manual work to 'white-collar' salaried employment, is changed in numerous important ways. Above all, these moves are generally felt to be forms of social improvement by those experiencing them.

A second important source of growth is the gain from what is

Table 2.2 Distribution of male labour in selected countries, *c.* 1950 and *c.* 1980, in per cent

	Agriculture		Manufacture, extractive		Services		Constructive, other	
	c.1950	1980	1950	1980	1950	1980	1950	1980
Austria	25	8	34	38	27	41	14	13
Belgium	14	4	45	31	34	52	7	13
France	33	9	27	30	32	48	8	13
Germany (West)	23	5	39	42	29	41	9	12
Italy	42	10	24	31	24	42	10	17
UK	7	3	45	36	39	50	9	11

Source: B. R. Mitchell (1992) *International Historical Statistics: Europe 1750–1988*: Basingstoke

known as the 'economies of scale'. In many industries and forms of transport, savings in cost per unit can be made if the scale of production or throughput goes up. To cite some obvious examples, it costs little more to produce 10,000 copies of a book than 5,000, so that average costs for the lot go down sharply when the print run is increased. Similarly, the extra costs of carrying 600 rather than 300 passengers on a train are negligible, so that the cost per passenger falls sharply with increased use. Rising output itself brought many such benefits: the falling real costs (bearing the effects of inflation in mind) of such things as cars or colour television sets are well known. For some industries, and for small countries, the home markets are so restricted that the full benefits of some scale economies can be achieved only if foreign markets as well can be tapped. Growth of this kind is therefore associated with the expansion of international trade, which will be discussed further in the next chapter. This, in turn, depends on good means of transport and communications as well as on a smooth system of making international payments, and on altogether more complex sets of economic relationships.

All these factors refer essentially to advanced industrial countries which have the wherewithal, given a framework of reasonable prosperity, to achieve a growth of a few percentage point per annum. The problems of the developing countries, and particularly of the poorer ones among them, are of quite a different order. The fact that they are so poor is proof that they lack at least some of the resources for growth. They frequently lack an entrepreneurial class, as well as a political framework favourable to exercise entrepreneurship; they lack skilled cadres of people; and the gap in technology and productivity is so great, that they cannot normally hope to bridge it with their own resources, particularly as the target of catching up with the industrial world is moving away from them all the time. They therefore depend not only on foreign expertise but also on foreign capital; since they usually have but one or a small number of export commodities, they also depend on favourable world markets for these. Within their limited possibilities, they have the kind of strategic choices to make which advanced countries are spared, such as whether they should go for an export drive or for import substitution as the channel for growth.

On the other hand, given reasonably favourable conditions, they have the chance of very rapid growth, because of the enormous gap in technology between them and the technical possibilities of the age. The larger the gap, the more rapid the growth, once it begins to be bridged, though in principle this could be easier for countries already fairly advanced than for the least developed. The possibility of bridging the gap between their own technology and the best available in the lead country, the USA, was in fact one of the causes of the very rapid economic growth of European continental countries from the 1950s, and of Japan somewhat later. By contrast, the leading economy, which in our period was mostly the United States, though lately they were joined by Japan, can grow only as fast as new technical progress permits.

TECHNOLOGICAL INNOVATION

Technological innovation and improvement, in the widest sense, have been the basic, and in many ways the most important source of economic growth in the modern world, more pervasive than the other two causes listed, structural change and economies of scale. Included here are not merely better machines or chemical processes and the like, but also improved organization and economic structure, and improvement in the quality, including the skills and flexibility, of labour.

Technological innovation is by its nature unpredictable and erratic; it varies widely in its impact, and affects individual industrial sectors differently and at different times. Nevertheless, out of the mix of possible technical improvements, there has in the post-war years emerged something like a regular growth possibility of 2½ per cent per annum. It is sometimes known as the 'underlying' growth rate, not quite achieved in depression years, but overshot, to return to the long-term growth path, in boom years. International trade helps to diffuse the technical advances made in one country to the rest of the world: thus all of us have benefited from the colour TV sets and cameras produced more efficiently in Japan, or from the ingenious German machine tools bought on the market in our period.

Improvements occurred in the quality of products as well as in their manufacture. The motor car, one of the most important products of the second half of the twentieth century, may serve as an example. Older members of the community can still remember the standard post-war models, with their starting handles to be inserted in the front, their separately mounted lamps, the inner tubes, the winking indicators, the single windscreen wiper, for the driver only, with heaters considered a luxury addition. The car of the 1990s, of which the invisible mechanical parts have changed just as much since 1950 as these external components, is practically a different product, and even if quantities produced had not changed, the quality differences alone would represent a substantial economic growth.

But quantities did change enormously. World output of passenger cars alone, not counting commercial vehicles, is shown in Figure 2.1. At the same time, the number of cars registered per thousand population had risen from 109 in 1960 to 245 in 1980 in Britain, from 122 to 290 in France and from 81 to 289 in Germany; in the USA meanwhile, it had reached 495. One might have thought that that figure, one car for every two persons of all ages, represented saturation, but car ownership has none the less been relentlessly rising since then: by 1991, it had reached 567 per thousand in the USA. The comparable growth in the number and capacity of commercial vehicles, such as trucks and buses, which rose on a world scale from 100 million in 1982 to 141 million in 1991 may be counted as part of the expansion of capital equipment which helped to raise productive efficiency for the economy as a whole. There has also been a corresponding extension of the road network, of car ferries and their terminals, of repair garages and filling stations and a growth in the output of producers of car components scattered among many industries.

There has also been a sea change in the structure of the motor car industry itself. After the war, the USA produced 79.5 per cent of the world's vehicles, or almost four times as much as the rest of the world put together. By 1975 this had dropped to 31.1 per cent and by 1991 to a mere 16.9 per cent. At first Europe increased its relative share, but then Japan took over, finally exceeding the American output, at least in numbers, by a considerable margin.

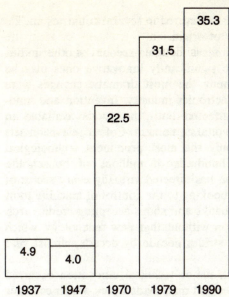

Figure 2.1 World output of passenger cars, 1937–1990, in millions

Thus in 1991 Japan turned out 9,775,000 vehicles, or 28.5 per cent of the world's total, as against the 5,441,000 which rolled off the American production lines. But Japan's share has recently been threatened in turn by such producers as Korea and Mexico, with 1,132,000 and 730,000 units in 1991 respectively. Whereas at one time car production was limited to a few advanced economies, motor vehicles have now come to be produced in well over two dozen countries, and are being assembled in many more, including numerous Third World countries. Most of these assembly plants are, however, owned or controlled by the great western and Japanese firms.

In structure, the industry is dominated by large firms which widespread amalgamations in the past half-century have made even larger. The largest twelve companies now produce between them some four-fifths of the world's total. It is considered that in order to gain full advantage from economies of scale, a maker would have to produce at least a million vehicles a year: if this estimate is correct, only the world's ten largest companies qualify. These giants have long since learnt to site some of their plants abroad in the search for cheap labour or to beat tariff barriers. This fact, together with the diffusion of specialist component suppliers, means that most cars are made up of parts manufactured in several countries and no longer have a single country of origin.

Space does not permit a similarly detailed account of other industries, but some of the more significantly innovative ones may be mentioned very briefly. Among the most dramatic changes were those to be found in the electronics industry. Invention and innovation in this field, too, affected both the goods available to consumers and productive capital equipment. Colour television sets and word processors are only the most prominent technological marvels in daily use by hundreds of millions of households. Additionally, computerization has affected virtually every sector of the economy, from airplane booking to the control of machine tools or the daily transactions in banks and shops accepting credit cards. Our world could not function without that new technology, which is still advancing with giant strides decade by decade, almost year by year.

Yet another area in which major technical innovation occurred was the production of plastics and man-made fibres, which can now be made to possess almost any conceivable property and colouring, and suit almost any conceivable use. The chemical industry, together with medical research, was also responsible for a previously unimaginable range of pharmaceutical products. In the 1990s the first successes of genetic engineering were recorded: its impact is as yet difficult to foresee, though it is likely to be more significant in the medical than the productive industrial field.

The enormous changes brought about by technical advance were not limited to manufacturing and related industries. Revolutionary progress also occurred in transport. Aircraft existed in 1945, but their development into regular service provision by liners carrying up to 400 passengers each was scarcely imagined then. In 1993, British airports alone counted close on 114 million passengers passing through their gates. Among other technical achievements was the construction of lengthy tunnels under the sea, such as those which connect Japanese islands or the two sides of San Francisco Bay area, and the Channel tunnel linking Britain with the continent of Europe. In the provision of electrical energy, coal, oil and hydro-power have been joined by nuclear power, by natural gas and even by geothermic energy, as well as by solar heating and wind power. Total world consumption of energy is still rising, from 5,800 billion kilowatt hours in 1980 to 7,700 billion in 1991.

Nor has agriculture, often considered the most conservative of economic sectors, been left out. In the advanced world, machinery, chemical fertilizers and pest control, together with plant and animal breeding, have increased output, despite a substantial fall of persons employed, to an extent which has turned the problem of supply on its head. Nowadays it is the surpluses, and not a potential shortage, which are the problem in some parts of the world. The notorious butter mountain and wine lake of the European Community, together with payments made to farmers in Europe and North America *not* to grow certain crops are eloquent proofs.

The Third World was not quite so fortunate, but it, too, had a so-called 'green revolution' of its own. This involved careful selective breeding and adaptation of species to soil and climatic conditions, together with irrigation or drainage. It achieved striking results. Starting experimentally in Mexico in the 1950s, its success led to its rapid spread to the rest of Latin America, to South and East Asia and even to Africa in the following decade. With its help, total food production increased by 2.74 per cent a year in Latin America between 1955 and 1970, by 2.77 per cent in the Far East and by 2.49 per cent in Africa; for rice, the first object of the experimentation and the staple of more than half the world's poorer societies, the annual growth rates were a good deal higher still, namely 4.85, 2.84 and 3.40 per cent respectively for these three regions.

These rates were well above the rates of population increase, so that the home food supply was eased for these areas, taking them as a whole, in this period. Even in the face of the continuous increase in the world population, to be discussed further in Chapter 5 below, the world now has the means, and still sufficient spare acreage, to feed all of it adequately at a generous 3,000 calories per person per day, if only political and social organization were adequate to the task. The real problem is that they are not. Moreover, the satisfactory regional production increases noted here hide failures in some individual countries within those regions, and do not take full account of the effects of natural disasters such as floods or droughts which hit some of these areas from time to time.

It was noted above that the services as a group now employ well over half the working population in the industrialized countries, and they are still expanding. Clearly, productivity rises in that sector will have a particularly large impact on increases in the overall efficiency of an economy. They are, however, less easy to quantify directly, since there is no obvious weight or unit measure, such as tons of steel or numbers of cars produced per man-hour, of the kind which can be found in manufacturing. Changes in productivity in the services therefore tend to be commonly measured by rises in incomes of people employed in that sector, on the grounds that they would not be paid if they did not add appropriate values by their work.

There is no doubt that in some services technological improvement has added immensely to output: computers in offices in the place of manual typewriters or comptometers, television to multiply the numbers able to view a theatrical performance, microwaves in restaurant kitchens, or the array of technological marvels to help doctors to diagnose illnesses and prescribe cures or undertake surgical operations. On the other hand, in some other services output per person has turned out to be difficult to raise: this includes hairdressers, taxi drivers or teachers, though videotapes and other technical aids show every sign of multiplying the output of the individual teacher also.

INDUSTRIAL AND COMMERCIAL ORGANIZATION

Next to technological change in the narrow sense, there were also considerable changes in industrial and commercial organization. Some of these affected the internal management of factories, shipyards and mines. In 1945, the most advanced internal organization was still the mass-production system of the type first installed in its full extent by Henry Ford in his car plant just before World War I, and known as 'Fordism'. The essence of the Fordist system of production was careful planning and design in separate departments away from the shop floor, combined with the reduction of the manual work to easy, repetitive routine tasks as the work on the conveyor belt flowed past the labourer. Human skills were highly concentrated in the design departments, but removed, apart from repair and maintenance men, from the actual productive process: workers engaged in the latter quickly learnt their manual turns, and were otherwise unskilled and interchangeable.

To make all this possible, there had to be a massive investment in mechanical plant, which, in turn, required long production runs of identical goods. Given those conditions, Fordism was highly effective in increasing output and reducing costs, while providing, in many cases, reasonable wages for work which might be tedious, but for which time and motion studies could reduce the physical effort involved. Apart from motor cars it spread most rapidly in other mass-producing assembly industries, such as the making of radios, kitchen equipment, and later TV sets, cameras and the like. The cheapening of products which it achieved contributed a great deal to the rising standards of consumption of the age.

The system is still indispensable today in many industries, but its limits have become increasingly evident in the later decades of the twentieth century. Curiously enough, it was its very success in raising incomes and expectations which in the end showed up some of its weaknesses. It was replaced by alternatives in two directions. One had to do with the increased variety demanded by a more sophisticated and better-off public. While the Ford plant turned out identical 'model Ts', all of a black colour, modern car producers have to turn out units which differ not only in colour, but also in one of more than twenty possible attachments and varieties. In the most advanced systems, the orders for these, as reported by the dealers, can be co-ordinated by computerization which can alter and set machines accordingly, but it is clear that more adaptability and skill are required of the work force in such a framework of flexible production.

Industrial psychology has also pointed to the low level of morale and loyalty to the firm under Fordism, and some firms have therefore turned to batch production, in which each worker has a larger share in making the final product. Increasingly, also, manufacture has been transferred to smaller units, often in more pleasant locations than the huge plants of the mass producers, and offering greater variety of work as well as more flexible hours to suit female employees in particular. What may perhaps be considered an extreme form of this development is the growing practice of employing people who work for their firms in their own homes, possibly linked to head office by computer. This allows the employee the greatest amount of freedom to select his or her hours and working environment. It echoes in a curious way the practices of 'domestic industry' of the days before factory industrialization.

In view of the great success of Japanese industry since the war, of which more below, the internal organization in Japanese companies has attracted widespread attention in the rest of the world, on the general assumption that the causes of the astonishing rise in productivity in that country have to be found at least in part in that area. It has not, however, proved easy to grasp the essence of the Japanese system, if indeed there is one, still less to apply it elsewhere. It may well be that a long cultural tradition, strongly under the influence of China, has played a part, a suspicion confirmed by the fact that the equally successful 'Eastern Tigers' all either have large Chinese populations or, in the case of Korea, had long been under Chinese and Japanese cultural influence. If so, direct imitation would become all the more difficult.

As far as can be judged, the system or systems developed in Japan have some similarities with the more recent innovations in western industrial organization. Thus efforts of a psychological kind to induce a positive response of loyalty and feeling of belonging play an important part. In Japan these are aided by the promise of lifetime employment, at least for a worker élite, and by increases of pay and status with years of service, rather like in the civil service elsewhere. Workers, though possessed of skill, are expected to be flexible in their employment and, by being rotated among jobs, may be able to gain an insight into the workings of the whole plant and their particular part in it. They may also be called upon, more frequently than in the west, to help the management with advice and even influence decisions by giving advice based on their experience. Quality control has been given a high priority in the leading companies. Curiously enough, the latest technological needs are well served by the established 'kanban' system, in which production schedules are determined by market information reaching the plant upstream, as it were, leading incidentally to the opportunity of reducing the costly burden of large inventories of components and spare parts.

Finally, the declining significance of Fordist organization is also explained by the fact that mass-produced articles need localized and customer-friendly service and repair stations. These, too, are based on flexibility, on skill and on personal contact. They may be taken as one aspect of the rising significance of the services in the economy. The organization of services as a whole has a logic of its own, and it is different from that of Fordism.

While there are many humdrum and repetitive jobs to be found in the services, most of them require some initiative or adaptability on the part of those working in them, in addition to trained skills in the traditional sense. Most of the learned professions are to be found in that sector, as well as jobs involving adaptability to meet the needs of individual customers. It is, in fact, the rising expectations of better-off consumers which have been at least in part responsible for the increased share of employment in the services. Among the most rapidly expanding service industries are financial services, retail distribution, teaching as school age is raised everywhere and numbers of students in tertiary education and among adults increase manyfold, and personal services in restaurants, hairdressing salons and the like. Some of the organizations providing these, such as banks, building and insurance societies and retailing chains, are among the largest enterprises in the industrialized countries, but it is clear that the logic of work in them, calling for constant initiative and flexibility, at least when face to face with the customer, is totally different from the logic of the wholly repetitive work out of sight of the consumer, on which the classic conveyor belt factory was based.

THE MULTINATIONALS

One of the more striking developments among the largest companies in the half-century since the end of World War II has been the expansion of their international connections. Virtually all large concerns are now 'multinational' or 'transnational': in other words, they have active branches in many countries, though there is usually an easily recognized head office and a single country of origin. The larger ones among them are remarkably widely spread: in 1976, it was found that the 371 multinationals which had branches in over 20 countries each, controlled three-fifths of all such branches. Recently there have been cases of hiving off some head offices to foreign locations: thus in 1991 DuPont moved the headquarters of their agricultural products division from the USA to Geneva, while IBM relocated the head office for their world-wide communication system to London.

Some multinational companies, defined in this way, were to be found even before 1914, and their number expanded greatly in the inter-war years. Their most rapid growth, however, has taken place since 1945. There are several reasons for this development. As noted above, some companies place factories to produce components or undertake certain stages of the manufacturing process abroad because of the cheap labour, but also because of cheaper raw materials or lower costs of energy there. They may also hope to find laxer legal restraints on the treatment of their labour, or on evironmental pollution. In some cases, they have had to establish mines or plantations abroad simply because the natural resource bases are found there.

They may also go abroad in search of additional markets. One aspect of this is the attempt to bypass tariff barriers or other methods of restricting imports. Thus the founding of numerous motor car factories by Japanese companies within Europe was at least in part a response to the attempts by European governments to limit their imports. In some cases, however, especially in the service industries, such as banking, insurance, car hire, fast food or retail distribution, companies such as Woolworth's or C & A, Hertz or MacDonald's, have to go abroad, because that is the only way to tap their foreign customers. Frequently the expansion of one firm into branches abroad provides a spur to its competitors to do likewise, in order not to lose ground in the race for market shares and scale economies. Contrary to widespread public opinion which holds multinationals, as a type, to be 'monopolistic', they commonly find themselves in tough competitive conditions. There are few industries in which competition is as fierce as among oil companies and motor car producers, both of which count some of the largest and most powerful multinationals among their number. At the same time they may collaborate in consortia even in those two competitive industries.

The actions of multinationals have been subjected to criticism on other grounds, too. In the industrialized countries, they are said to exercise control over employment without social or political responsibility: in times of depression they may pull out, leaving the social costs to be borne by others. They avoid taxes by manipulating the prices with which branches invoice each other so as to show profits only in the country with the lowest taxes. This, in turn, distorts export and import figures, tariff protection and subsidy measures in the host countries.

In non-industrialized countries, particularly the smaller ones, they are accused of wielding an unacceptable degree of power, being frequently in a position to influence or blackmail local or central government by threats or bribery: oil companies, mining companies and exporters of agricultural products are most commonly accused of these obnoxious practices. Some multinationals, indeed, control budgets larger than those of many sovereign countries. Thus in 1991, six companies had turnovers of over 50 billion ECU each: these were General Motors, Royal Dutch Shell, Exxon, Ford, IBM and Toyota.

Yet multinationals are often highly efficient and among the technical leaders and innovators. Where they are subject to competition, they pass on most of the gains arising therefrom to consumers: they have been responsible for much of the increase in output and productivity noted at the beginning of this chapter. They have helped to introduce up-to-date, frequently American, practices, know-how and capital into other industrialized countries, and have had a hand in helping towards the 'convergence' of European economies catching up with the American leaders. In less advanced countries

Table 2.3 Multinational companies in 1973

Country of origin	Number of companies	260 largest multinational companies Number employees, Million	
USA	2,567	126	11.8
United Kingdom	1,588	49	4.0
West Germany	1,222	21	2.8
Switzerland	765	5	0.4
France	565	19	2.1
Netherlands	467	6	1.2
Japan	211	9	0.6
Rest of world	2,096	25	2.2
Total world	9,481	260	25.1

Source: Neil Wood and Stephen Young (1979) *The Economics of Multinational Enterprise*, London, pp. 17, 23

those effects have commonly been even more powerful. There, the multinationals have frequently also brought in much needed capital. If they pay low wages for long hours of work, compared with those ruling in the mother countries, it has to be borne in mind that without them, wages would be lower still and employment more restricted. Foreign companies have frequently contributed most effectively to raising the general wage level within the host community. Curiously enough, some critics make the opposite complaint that they tend to neglect these regions in favour of investing in the more familiar conditions of the developed industrialized countries. By 1975, it has been alleged, only 26 per cent of their direct foreign investment was made in the Third World.

Immediately after the war, as was to be expected, it was the multinationals of American origin which expanded fastest: by 1966, there were nearly 9,000 American subsidiaries in western Europe alone. Britain, building largely on her pre-war foundations, especially in Commonwealth countries, came next, followed by the other leading industrial and colonial nations, as shown in Table 2.3. By 1989, the hundred largest companies were employing 12 million people outside the borders of their home country.

Japan, it will be seen, came low down the list: there were in fact several countries with more companies than Japan at the time, that have been omitted from the table. Since then, however, Japanese multinationals have taken their place among the leaders.

In addition to the giant companies, smaller units and even individuals have expanded their holdings of foreign assets which remain

Table 2.4 Foreign direct investment, selected countries, 1967–1990

	1967		1990	
	FDI US $bn	% GDP	FDI US $bn	% GDP
USA	56.6	7.1	426.5	7.9
United Kingdom	15.8	14.5	244.8	25.1
Japan	1.5	0.9	201.4	6.8
W. Germany	3.0	1.6	155.1	10.4
World total	112.3	4.0	1,644.2	8.0

Source: J. H. Dunning (1993) *The Globalization of Business:* London, p. 288

under their control, known as 'foreign direct investment'. Putting all kinds together, Japan's direct foreign investment has expanded enormously, fed in part by Japan's technological lead, by her need to get over hostile tariff barriers, and by her enormous payment surpluses which were available to be invested abroad. Between 1988 and 1995 it grew at the rate of 15 per cent per annum, compared with 10 per cent for France and Germany, and much less for the USA and the United Kingdom.[3] Not unnaturally, the geographical distribution of overseas investment by the Japanese differed from that of their western counterparts. Much the largest share went to the United States, but thereafter a great effort went into Asia and Latin America. The annual resource transfer from Japan to the USA increased from US $18 bn in 1983 to US $40 bn in 1993, and to Europe from US $8 bn to US $19 bn in the same years. As elsewhere, most of the investments were made by the giant multinational companies: in 1978, Mitsui led, with 247 bn yen invested in branches abroad, followed by Mitsubishi, Marubeni, Itoh and Sumitomo. These were the leading conglomerates, the famous *zaibatsu*, which had been modified only slightly in the democratization drive after the war into *keiretsu*. One Japanese speciality, however, was the grouping of smaller companies in '*sogo sosha*' within networks of larger concerns for the purpose of overseas expansion. Some comparative details, of 'foreign direct investment', are shown in Table 2.4.

It should be noted that despite its growth in terms of dollars, the American capital export as a proportion of national income changed but little. The largest relative increase was registered by Japan, for which the figures have since doubled once more. In the United Kingdom, the high rate of growth was accounted for in part by the investment of the oil revenues, and was largely matched by an increase in inward investment by foreign companies. As a proportion of national income invested abroad, the Netherlands and Switzerland had the highest rates. Inward investment was highest in the USA, the UK, Germany and Latin America.

NEGATIVE ASPECTS OF GROWTH

To conclude this chapter on the growth of production and productivity in the half-century 1945–95, some negative aspects of that growth must be considered. The greatly expanded production per head, accompanied as it was by a more than doubling of the world's population, necessarily strained the resources of the globe, quite apart from the environmental effects, which will be described in Chapter 5 in our discussion of changes in the standard of living. Here we are concerned with the possible depletion of the resources used by man. They may be roughly grouped into minerals, sources of energy, and other animal and vegetative resources.

The supply of minerals has rarely been put in question, though they belong to the category of non-reproducible resources. Some metals, like iron ore and aluminium, are found almost everywhere, and iron represents over 90 per cent of all metals used. In the case of some others, such as tin or gold, producers have been concerned to limit supplies by official and unofficial restrictive schemes in order to keep up their price, rather than be troubled by shortages. Though in individual areas the ores may give out, there is no immediate danger of coming to the end of supplies. New finds may well require higher costs to mine and process in the future, but this will be counteracted to a greater or lesser extent by the technical innovations which may be expected. Recently, schemes for recycling some of the rarer metals have been started in the industrialized countries.

Coal, sometimes considered a mineral though of vegetable origin, was a main source of energy before 1945, especially in the richer countries. In regions where it was mined, it generally supplied, directly or in the form of gas or electricity, more than 90 per cent of energy requirements. Since then not merely its share, but even its absolute output, has been drastically curtailed: by 1980, it had dropped to 20 per cent of world energy sources, as against 47 per cent derived from oil and 18 per cent from natural gas. Taking into account only the known reserves, coal supplies at the present rate of consumption are calculated to last 232 years. Rather than coming up against any supply restraint, mines all over the industrialized world lie derelict and unwanted, their capital wasted, the miners unemployed. Much of what is still produced has to be subsidized to be sold, in order to stand up to competition from the other sources of energy as well as from eastern European mines and from supplies from such areas as Columbia.

In place of coal, the leading energy source now is oil, together with natural gas. In 1980, the world's natural gas reserves were calculated at 50 years' supply at the then rate of consumption, and this had increased by 1992 to 68 years' supply, though consumption had meanwhile gone up by one-half.

The rise of oil supplies was more dramatic. It has replaced coal in part because of its cheapness, but in part also because it is more convenient for the rapidly expanding demands by cars, airplanes and ships, as well as a base for plastics, synthetic rubber and the like. Before the war, the leading oil supply regions were the USA, the Soviet Union and Mexico; since then, the Middle East, including Iran, Algeria and Libya, has taken the lead, supplying around one-half of the world's oil, with Indonesia and Venezuela, and lately also West Africa, Britain and Norway rising in importance, while the USA turned into a major importer from 1968 onward. World output doubled between 1945 and 1950, it doubled again to 1960 and doubled once more, to 2,000 million tons in 1968.

The expectation was that it would double yet again within the next decade, but in 1973 that growth was suddenly halted by the OPEC price rise, enforced as it was by output restrictions by the leading suppliers. OPEC (the Organization of Petroleum Exporting Countries) had been formed in 1960, mainly to strengthen the hands of the governments of the poorer oil suppliers against the powerful multinational oil companies. In 1973, partly as a riposte to the Israeli military victory over her Arab neighbours, it used its near-monopoly power to increase the price of crude oil fourfold, followed by yet another large increase in 1979. Some of the consequences of this move for the world economy will be discussed in later chapters; here we may note that the industrialized world, faced by these huge price rises, was shown to be capable of effecting quite impressive fuel economies.

Since the onset of industrialization, greater efficiency had meant not merely rising output, but also the saving of energy. Thus it has been calculated that the energy requirement in the USA per $1,000 of real GDP, measured in tons of oil equivalents, has dropped steadily from 4.36 in 1850 to 1.47 in 1978 and is still falling. For a time, in 1973–4, world oil demand fell back sharply. It has since returned to its former rate, stabilizing at an output of around 60 million barrels a day between 1980 and 1993. OPEC power has been curbed by occasional defectors from the monopoly restrictions, and by new sources of supply: the share of OPEC has fallen steadily from 51 per cent in 1970 to 41 per cent in 1993. For the time being, the new deposits of oil discovered in the world as a whole are more than keeping pace with its rate of depletion, total known reserves having risen from 641 billion barrels in 1979 to 999 billion barrels at the end of 1993. There is therefore no shortage in sight, though ultimately the supply is bound to be finite. The resources of shale oil exceed those of mineral oil more than a hundredfold, and economical ways may well be found to extract it in the future.

It is into the third type of resource, mainly food and timber supply, that the most serious inroads have been made by increased consumption. Worst affected are the world's fishing grounds, as world catches have risen from 77 million tonnes in 1982 to 100 m.t. in 1989, with a slight fall since then. The whale population has been depleted to a dangerously low level and has had to be protected by international agreements, only inadequately enforced. Other heavily fished regions, including the ocean off Newfoundland, the North Sea and the Mediterranean, are also in grave danger of depletion by over-fishing, in spite of formal agreements to limit catches. From the Aral Sea in Russia all twenty-four species of fish once caught commercially are believed extinct; the Caspian yields only 1 per cent of the quantity of sturgeon caught fifty years ago.

On land, over-cropping leading to 'dust bowl' effects, as known earlier in the USA, or desertification, has been seen at its most destructive in the African Sahel region. Some 30 million people are affected, as the desert advances on the fertile land surrounding it at the rate of something like 100,000 hectares (250,000 acres) a year. Rising population numbers and their increased demands are largely responsible for over-cropping by farmers and over-grazing by increased numbers of herds and flocks; even the deeper wells sunk recently to provide much-needed water have come to be of little help, since they immediately lead to over-use of the land surrounding them. Thus years of drought, such as those of 1968 and 1970–2, lead to famines such as that of 1973, in which as many as 100,000 people died of starvation or disease. Production of cereals, in kilogram per person per year, had fallen from 223 in 1961–5 to only 153 in 1979 in the region, and even including imports, the available quantities have dropped from 241 kg to 189 kg per person.[4] Ethiopia is another country in which food supply is so finely balanced that the periodic droughts have led to widespread starvation.

Equally harmful in its consequences has been the destruction of forests, especially the rain forests of Brazil, Africa and parts of Asia. Since 1950 almost one-half of the Central American forest has disappeared, and one-third of the African one. This loss has been induced both by the world's voracious appetite for timber, and the search for land that may be turned to arable or grazing after the trees are removed. World output has risen by two-and-a-half times from 1,320 million cubic metres of round wood in 1948 to 2,929 million in 1982 and 3,429 million in 1991. Though theoretically reproducible, as new trees can be planted where old ones have been cut down, the complete clearing of large areas of woodland leads to erosion of the soil by wind and water, making new growth impossible. In some areas, such as Bangladesh, devastating floods in the lowlands may also follow as a result. The oxygen exchange which plants perform and which is vital to animal life, is also affected by the large-scale loss of forests.

By the late 1960s, the widespread misgivings among scientists over the effects of increased pressure on the world's resources, were brought into focus by the meetings of the Club of Rome in which numerous leading experts took part from 1968 onwards. Influential publications such as the Meadows' *The Limits to Growth*[5] alerted a wider public. Much of this was concerned with pollution, but some also referred to resource depletion. It has been shown since then that many of the fears expressed at the time were exaggerated, and that more or less effective action had been taken in various parts of the world. Nevertheless, the problems are real enough. Rising production for a rapidly growing world population has not taken place without costs, and the depletion of resources, especially of agricultural land in some regions, of fish stocks and timber supplies, were some of the hidden costs not always given their full due.

3 Trade and finance

FOREIGN TRADE

The high and rising productivity described in the last chapter was achieved in part by increasing specialization or division of labour. Some form of economic specialization has existed from the dawn of history: farmers supplied food to townspeople, makers of textile goods exchanged their products against metal objects through the market, and so on. In recent decades, the division of labour has become much more extensive, sophisticated and efficient.

Specialization requires trade. As the consumer, having earned his or her wage or salary, prepares to spend it in the shops, there has had to be simultaneously a stream of goods from numerous producers and intermediaries reaching the shopkeeper to stock his shelves ready for the eager spenders. Behind the selection which meets the eye of the consumer lies a vast network of trade. Most of this trade originates from within the country, but some crosses the borders and becomes foreign trade. As a general rule, the proportion of national income traded abroad is greater in a small economy than in a large country, in which more specialization is possible *within* the borders; it has also been found that more advanced countries trade more intensively than non-industrialized ones. For all of them external trade forms only a proportion of the total: yet far more of the attention of economists and economic policy makers has always been devoted to it than to internal commerce. In much of the literature and discussion on policy, 'trade' simply means external trade.

In our period, foreign trade has grown enormously. It has grown a good deal faster than GNP: in other words, a larger share of output is sent across the frontiers. Owing to the disruptions of war, the volume of trade stagnated between 1936–8 (index number 106

Table 3.1 Changes in world commodity trade, 1980–1992

	(Values) Average annual rate of growth, %	Share in world merchandise exports, %
Food	3.8	9.6
Fuels	−2.8	9.1
Iron and steel	2.5	2.8
Chemicals	7.2	9.0
Machinery and transport equipment	8.3	37.3
(of which automotive products)	8.8	9.9
Textiles	6.5	3.2
Clothing	10.2	n.a.

Source: UN, *World Economic and Social Survey*

at 1913 = 100) and 1948 (index 103); but thereafter it shot up, the index for visible trade reaching 520 in 1971. While world trade between 1948 and 1971 grew at the rate of 7.27 per cent a year, world industrial output grew by only 5.6 per cent[1] and total GNP by less than 5 per cent; similarly, between 1991 and 1994 world output growth averaged 1.2 per cent per annum, while trade grew at the average rate of 4.7 per cent. There were two major reasons for this faster growth: one derived from the fact that enhanced efficiency implies generally a greater degree of specialization and therefore a more than proportionate increase in the exchange of goods; the other, that in the years since World War II, many barriers to international trade have come down or have at least been lowered. The latter development is discussed in some detail in Chapter 6: here we turn to the link between economic progress and trade.

As might be expected, not all goods shared equally in the general growth of merchandise trade. The divergent experience of some important groups of commodities in recent years is illustrated in Table 3.1.

There was less room for the trade in the more traditional commodities to increase, either because, as in the case of food, world consumption increased very little, once a certain level of incomes had been reached, or, as in the case of textiles and fuels, because much of the international division of labour had been long established and needed little adjustment. By contrast, commodities whose consumption was rising rapidly with rising incomes, or those connected with the ever-increasing capital investment and complexities of production, such as machinery, chemicals and motor cars, showed the fastest rise. This applied particularly to goods for which much of the world's output was concentrated in a few countries, like machinery, electronic goods and cars, or where there was a significant transfer of the location of production, as in the case of clothing, much of which has now been shifted from high-wage to low-wage countries.

Traditionally, and right up to World War II, much of long-distance trade had consisted of the export of primary commodities, such as food and raw materials, from Third World, or 'developing' countries, to the rich, industrial countries in Europe, North America and Japan, in return for the manufactured goods, as well as services such as finance and transport, which the latter were best able to supply. Some of that pattern still holds, but our period has seen significant, almost startling, changes in this respect. Above all, there has been a most striking increase in the proportion of manufactured goods among the exports of the developing countries. Between 1980 and 1991, that proportion for all developing countries as a group rose from 19.5 per cent to 40.1 per cent; but for Indonesia it rose from 2.4 per cent to 30.8 per cent; and for West Asia, from 4.5 per cent to 14.5 per cent. The proportion of the more traditional primary goods, other than fuels, exported by these countries, changed but little, falling from 16.9 per cent to 14.7 per cent of the total, or to less than half the fraction representing manufactured exports: the big fall occurred among fuels, which were reduced from 32.4 per cent to 9.4 per cent for the group as a whole, largely because of the relative fall in the price of oil from its high point of 1979–80.

The stagnation, and in fact slight relative decline in the export of primary commodities from the developing countries had several causes. For one thing, the industrialized world's need for raw materials has not grown in step with incomes, as progress came to mean better and more complex and sophisticated, rather than simply more goods. Secondly, the consumption, and therefore the trade, in food has increased by less than GNP as a whole. Moreover, the greater ability of the industrialized countries to grow their own food and to substitute some raw materials, such as rubber or natural fibres, by synthetic ones made at home has reduced the commerce in these articles. By contrast, the successful onset of industrialization in the developing world, partly on the basis of the transfer of some of the more routine manufacturing work to it by the multinationals, has raised the share of industrial products in its exports.

These changes may be taken to reflect progress of some kind; nevertheless, the developing countries are still dependent on the industrialized world for orders, for know-how and for capital. They are also very vulnerable to changes in the prosperity of the richer countries. If these are in depression, the lack of orders communicates itself at once to the poorer regions of the globe, which may suffer a disproportionate decline in their incomes, while their obligations to 'service' the foreign capital, that is to say, to pay interest and repay some of the borrowings, remains. In fact, none of the changes listed here has made any inroads into the dominance of the developed market economies in international commerce. Sixty-three per cent of the world's exports went to them in 1960, rising to over 70 per cent in 1992. Most of the world's trade still consists of trade *among* the industrialized nations: of their own exports, 70 per cent went to other developed market economies in 1960, 71 per cent in 1980, and 75 per cent in 1992. Against that, in the latter year, only

- 2.4 per cent went to the 'economies in transition' (the former communist countries),
- 4.9 per cent to Latin America,
- 2.3 per cent to Africa,
- 3.3 per cent to West Asia, with a rather larger proportion,
- 9.8 per cent to the enormous populations of South and East Asia, and
- 1.2 per cent to China.

Much of the three-quarters of the world's foreign trade which is thus made up of trade among the industrially advanced nations consists of the exchange of similar manufactured goods. This is in stark contrast to the traditional pattern noted above, in which dissimilar goods were exchanged. The gains from the trade in that traditional pattern were likely to have been very large. Thus if Britain or Germany had been forced to grow all the bread grains consumed by their citizens instead of importing a portion of them from such regions as Canada, the USA, Russia or India, where they were being produced so much more cheaply, their own costs would have gone up and their incomes suffered correspondingly; at the same time, they would have lost some of the scale advantages of finding large markets for their manufactures among the food suppliers abroad in their return trade. By contrast, the gain to the present-day populations derived from exports of German cars to France, met in part by a similar stream of French cars to Germany, is likely to be very slight indeed. It may well be that the citizens of both countries could have found every conceivable model of vehicle and its variant purely among those manufactured within their own borders without having to go abroad for imports at all. The preference for the product of other countries was frequently quite irrational, based on clever advertising or unthinking tradition.

Thus, while there is still much gain to be derived from the growth of trade even among the advanced countries, because of the different resource bases, skills and enterprise existing in them, there have been only diminishing returns to be got in recent decades from this kind of division of labour. The gain from this type of trade is limited to the relatively small differences in costs between countries, *less* the costs of transport and of the foreign sales drive. The impression commonly given by powerful mercantilist and other nationalist propaganda that exports represent huge benefits to the economy, so that the boosting of exports thus becomes a major aim of policy, is to that extent misleading. The frequently cited benefits of export-led growth, or the widespread belief that the rapid economic recovery of the members of the European Economic Community in its earlier years was due to their rising inter-trade, are therefore less justified than is commonly thought: the benefits of trade are greatest where goods are exchanged which the trading partners could reproduce at home only at much greater cost or not at all.

BANKING AND FINANCE

International trade needs a particular type of banking and financial support. Banks have existed for hundreds of years in the advanced countries. Their main tasks have been to collect deposits of money from some members of the public in order to lend it to others or invest it at interest, to facilitate payments without having to handle cash, and to issue notes and other means of credit.

The needs of foreign trade were more complex and in the course of time banks specializing in exchange and overseas finance business evolved alongside the banks developed for domestic commerce. In the second half of the twentieth century the rise of multinational companies created a particular need for such facilities. In the event, not only was such an expanded system of banking provided to aid trade: it experienced a steeply rising development far beyond the needs of commerce and industry. By the 1980s and 1990s it had turned into a powerful and pervasive feature of the world's economic life in its own right. Both the development and the structure of this international financial sector are complex and they have been in constant flux over this period; they can be described only in the merest outline in these pages.

One important source of this internationalization or, as it is some-times called, 'globalization' of finance was the emergence of 'eurodollars' and 'eurocurrency'. Their origin was connected with the freeing of most European foreign exchange transactions in 1958, following the gradual removal of wartime controls (of which more in Chapter 7 below), while simultaneously in the USA the 'Q' regulation of the Federal Reserve Board set a ceiling to the interest that could be charged by banks and savings institutions. American holders then found that if they left their accounts in a British or other European bank, there was no restriction on the interest they could get. This was a direct incentive for them to transfer funds to non-USA, so-called 'offshore' banks, at first mainly to London. These dollar funds could then be lent, bought and sold without ever returning to the USA, while at the same time also escaping the restrictions which European governments put on their own nationals: the eurodollar was created. Before long other currencies came to be used away from home in a similar way: the euro-currencies.

Furthermore, the banks and finance houses in that international system of trading found that by using the Cayman Islands, the Bahamas or other tax havens, they could obtain the advantage of paying few or no taxes as well as escape other restrictions to which other banks were subject. In this manner, much of international finance became detached from any real industrial or economic base as had been the case with earlier banking. At the same time, new financial centres which did have a healthy economic base also grew into importance, partly engaging in international trade, including Tokyo, Hong Kong, Singapore and Sydney. London, however, remained the main market for this kind of finance.

Freed from all restrictions and most taxes, the system took off. From the not insignificant figure of US $5 billion in 1960, the euro-currency market rose twentyfold to US $110 billion in 1970 and then once again tenfold to the almost inconceivable sum of US $1,120 billion (US $610 billion net) in 1979. By the end of 1994, $2,062 billion in international bonds and $406 billion in euronotes were outstanding and the bonds issued in that year totalled $442 billion. Enormous sums were thus swirling round the world's money markets, out of control of the governmental monetary authorities, but also out of control of the original depositors, since much of the lending was organized by consortia or syndicates of banks and by other specialist intermediaries, two or three steps away from the actual owners of the assets.

Other organizations, even less solidly based, then arose to trade in, that is to say, to buy and sell, these funds: since they had to hold stocks of them, they had to finance these holdings by raising funds elsewhere – the so-called secondary market. In the 1990s, the market turned to so-called over-the-counter derivative investments, to hedge against price rises and other changes. This meant that markets became more inter-related, and disturbances would spread very fast across the system.

Moreover, a large proportion of the funds flowing into it had been lent on short term, but the loans provided were generally lent out at medium term (two to ten years) if not on long-term bonds ('eurobonds'): but borrowing short and lending long has always been considered a recipe for disaster in the financial world. Further, there was no central bank, no 'lender of last resort', such as protects or backs up banks and their customers within each of the advanced countries, and no supervision to prevent or detect undue risk-taking with other people's money. In consequence, the system was highly volatile, following in a frantic manner expected or rumoured exchange-rate or interest-rate alterations, rushing into rising markets and departing from expected falling ones, and thereby gravely exaggerating the impact of every change or expected change. While the players in it could make large profits by small changes on large turnovers, they had to be ever fearful of untoward or unpredictable events which would turn these into large losses. Much of this activity had little or nothing to do with the real economic or industrial life of the countries concerned, yet it was at times gravely affecting their prosperity.

As for the source of funds, apart from the United States, much of them originated in the early stages in Switzerland, but later also in Germany and then in other surplus economies, including Japan. Thirty-five per cent of the international bonds issued in 1994 were denominated in US dollars, 18.4 per cent in yen and 9.4 per cent in Deutschmark, the remainder in other currencies.

Who borrowed these sums? In the 1970s and 1980s, much of the lending was destined for Third World countries, hard hit by the OPEC oil price increases and the world depression which they triggered. The unwisdom of lending enormous sums to these economies, particularly in Latin America, very soon became evident in the major world debt crisis which was the result. It is referred to further in Chapter 6. But the dire effects of decisions taken by financiers could be felt even in Europe. A determined 'run' by the speculators on a currency, or a speculative flight into it, would defeat the counter-measures even of the government of one or more large countries to keep a currency stable. Examples were the 'black days', such as the pound's 'black Wednesday' on 16 September 1992, when it was forced out of the European Exchange Rate Mechanism despite the most determined and costly effort of the Treasury to stem the tide. There has thus arisen in the world a financial power, even if a diffuse one not under any single control, to rival and at times defeat the economic policies devised by democratic governments.

Also, since funds and players have come to be based all over the globe, it has become difficult if not impossible to find out, in the case of fraud, where the crimes were committed, who committed them or where to begin to pick up the pieces. The classic case of the most far-reaching swindle of the age was associated with the collapse of the BCCI bank, which had operated in sixty-nine countries, in July 1991, but there were many others. Even the banks themselves may nowadays lose control, as in the case of the Baring scandal of 1995, in which unwise and uncontrolled gambling rather than fraud led to the collapse of Britain's oldest bank with losses of £700 million.

Globalization, that ugly word, also means that there is a tendency for interest rates, duly modified by degrees of risk, to be aligned with each other the world over. Similarly, the sequences of booms and slumps become ever more synchronized on a global scale through the financial mechanism. This, again, weakens the power of individual countries to stem the tide or buck the trend according to their own priorities. At the same time, the 'market', or the consensus of the players in it, has been found to be efficient in spotting weaknesses which governments have been trying to hide, and forcing countries to take appropriate corrective measures.

CAPITAL EXPORTS

Included within these footloose flows between lenders and borrowers are the more solid capital exports from one country to another. Some of this movement, as it affected the multinational companies, has been referred to in Chapter 2 above, but foreign investment which was not tied to internal company policies has also greatly increased and partly changed direction in our period.

It is a complex issue, not easily penetrated. Foreign investment, or sending capital abroad, may be looked at from three angles. First, there must be a surplus of savings which savers, or organizations like investment trusts acting for them, are willing to invest abroad.

It will therefore be found that people in countries which are net foreign investors, that is, for which the capital flowing out is larger than the sums flowing in, generally save a large share of their incomes, though there are some contrary cases of capital flight, caused by the fact that a country's own credit is so dubious that savers are reluctant to put their money there. Second, the regions to which the investments flow must offer reasonable propositions to savers: this could mean government or local government loans; it may mean investment in local companies; or it may mean the establishment of new companies under foreign control – at which point we approach the tactics of the multinationals.

But third, the sum of these decisions to send their money abroad that have been taken by numerous individuals, emerges on the national scale as a transmission of funds which have to be ultimately financed by a national payments surplus achieved elsewhere. If, as an example, German investors in their individual capacity or through their companies have taken decisions which amount, in the end, to the transmission of $1 billion of capital abroad, the German economy must have created a payments surplus in other areas, for example by exporting more goods, to finance that sum and thus balance the books. Otherwise, if the investments are made ultimately by borrowing the money abroad, there will be technically a foreign investment into Germany to balance the German investment outward, and there will have been no German *net* investment.

All this means that it is countries which are in surplus in current trading which originate foreign investment, and those in deficit which receive it. Thus, measured in billions of US dollars, German net foreign lending averaged 0.2 in 1985–9 and 7.9 in 1990–3; the corresponding figures for Japan were 20.3 and 11.8, while for the USA there was an *inflow* of 3.4 and 11.4 respectively in those years. While much foreign investment had gone into the Third World up to the early 1980s, thereafter an astonishingly large proportion was directed into the USA, until the early 1990s, when some of the traditional flows were resumed. Capital movements, especially those originating from Japan, thus helped to balance out the American payments deficit on current account: the Japanese resource transfer to the USA averaged US $30.9 billion per annum in the years 1991–3, with a rising tendency.

America is in a special position in this respect. While any other country subject to the enormous current payments deficits which the USA has sustained in the past thirty years would have seen its credit diminish and the value of its currency wiped out, the

Americans could continue to borrow abroad in this way because of the particular position of the US dollar. In the post-war years it had been the leading reserve currency, that is, the currency in which the central banks of other countries held their reserves to meet international obligations. The dollar kept that status even after the relative economic power of the USA had been weakened as the central banks as well as the citizens of other countries continued to be quite willing to hold dollars, and trade with them. Not least, the world's oil is traded in dollars.

Some of these issues will be discussed further in Chapter 7. Here we might merely take note of the fact that capital movements in one direction lead in due course to remittances, which have to be financed by export surpluses, in the other direction as interest payments and capital repayments become due. This was one major aspect of the world's debt crisis which will be described in Chapter 6 below.

4 The changing geography of economic activity

THE INDUSTRIALIZED WESTERN WORLD

The preceding three chapters contained a number of scattered references to the varying experiences of different regions of the globe. It is time to look at the picture as a whole by tracing the changing geographical distribution of the world's economic activity in its broad divisions.

We may begin with the leading economy, the United States, to which Canada may be added for many purposes. Completely dominant in 1945, the USA owed her favourable position not merely to the damage and destruction suffered by her leading rivals in the war, but also to her technical and commercial superiority which had been clearly established well before 1939, as well as to her immense natural resources. Even in 1971, by which time others had made much progress, the USA still accounted for a third of world industrial production. In terms of output per worker in manufacturing, it was calculated for 1967 that if the USA is taken as 100, Germany stood at 50, Japan and France at 45 and Britain at 35.[1] At the same time, agricultural labour productivity was many times higher than that in other advanced countries not merely because of superior technology, but also because the number of acres per person exceeded those available in Europe and Japan by an enormous margin.

There were two major reasons why some of that lead was eroded in the course of the half-century to 1996. One might be called political. Having taken on the mantle of political leadership in the western world, the USA saw itself as the leading military power, not merely in the struggle against communism in major wars such as those of Korea and Vietnam, but also in numerous other conflicts, especially in the rest of the western hemisphere and in Africa. In addition to an enormous armaments programme in the USA itself, the Cold War also led to large expenditure on espionage and subversion abroad, and on propping up weak or dubious governments to keep them within the western orbit. More positively, the USA also supported her allies in Europe by economic aid through the Marshall Plan, of which more in Chapter 6, and was the leading contributor, directly and through international organizations, to the provision of aid and loans to the poorer countries of the Third World. These activities not merely reduced the funds which might otherwise have been available for investment and consumption in the USA, but were a major cause of the American payments deficit from the 1950s onwards. It might well be said that what had happened was that the USA had converted some of her riches into political power and influence.

Second, to the extent that American technology could be copied, the countries in the rest of the industrialized world, including above all Europe, the Soviet Union and Japan, were in a position and had the capability to do so. Some of the copying was initiated by governments, helped by the USA authorities eager to build up economic bulwarks against the Soviet Union; some was undertaken by private concerns; some was transferred abroad by American transnational companies; and some was engineered by industrial spies, particularly those working for the USSR and her allies. Catching up with American technology was possibly the outstanding industrial development of the age on the part of the advanced world.

In this, the imitators were trying to hit a moving target, as that technology was being constantly improved, not least by scientists, technologists and inventors who flocked from all parts of the world to the USA as the most promising and progressive economy. Whilst, therefore, the USA lost some ground in the 1950s and 1960s, when the GNP of most European countries grew at 5–6 per cent a year, and that of Japan rose much faster, compared with the 3–4 per cent range of the USA, the latter still kept a wide lead. Comparative productivity data are shown in Table 4.1.

In the 1980s and 1990s growth elsewhere slowed down, in part because the technological boundary was being approached, henceforth merely keeping pace with the American growth which continued at its wonted rate. The American share of world output was still 27 per cent in 1990. In 1993, GDP per capita (at US dollars of 1988) had reached $20, 521 in the USA as against an average of $15,063 in the European Union. Japan, according to the same United Nations statistics, then stood at $26,864, well above the USA, but

Table 4.1 Productivity per man-hour, 1950–1979 (in US $ of 1970)

	1950	1970	1979
USA	4.25	6.96	8.28
Canada	3.33	5.96	7.03
Germany	1.40	4.62	6.93
France	1.85	4.92	7.11
United Kingdom	2.40	4.27	5.48
Japan	0.59	2.79	4.39

Source: Angus Maddison (1982) *Phases of Capitalist Development*: Oxford and New York, p. 212

this figure was somewhat artificial, derived from the high value of the Japanese yen. On a comparison of purchasing power, Japan's product per head was then still only 84.3 per cent of the American level.

Within western Europe, four broad groups of countries may be distinguished. Switzerland and Sweden, both neutral in the war, started with a high post-war productivity figure, then kept up with the leaders on the basis of a respectable annual growth rate. The second group consisted of the bulk of the industrialized nations of the continent, including France, Germany, Italy, the remaining Scandinavian countries, Belgium, the Netherlands and Austria. These as a group showed astonishingly high growth rates, with certain individual differences, until the early 1970s. Germany's rapid recovery, to become once more Europe's leading economy, is sometimes referred to as an 'economic miracle', but the thorough modernization of France and the breakthrough which turned Italy into a highly successful industrial economy seemed equally miraculous.

The third group consisted of the United Kingdom, together with the Irish Republic. The UK started from a level well above that of the countries in the second group, but had an economic growth rate so low as to be completely out of line with her neighbours; in consequence, she had dropped well behind by the end of the period, as seen in Table 4.1 above. Lastly, southern Europe, comprising Spain, Portugal, Greece and possibly Turkey, had been in the past at a much lower level altogether, but made rapid strides in the 1980s, though (apart from Turkey) they suffered badly in the recession of the early 1990s. They are still a good deal poorer, and less industrialized, than the European average.

JAPAN AND THE FAR EAST

If there was a real miracle, it was surely the rise of Japan from defeat and impoverishment to become the second industrial power of the world. Much has already been said about that country in earlier chapters. Here we may stress additionally her exceptionally poor natural endowment: since she possesses very limited agricultural land (four-fifths of the country being too mountainous to be worked), and had to import her oil, her minerals including iron ore, as well as, early on, her technology, her success is all the more astonishing. In the course of her transformation, her main export industries switched from textiles to capital goods such as steel and ships, to motor cars and to high-tech electronic and similar products.

A whole library of books has been written to account for the success of that oriental power in beating the west at its own game. Many works have been composed with the object of providing advice to others hoping to tread the same path. While we cannot follow these speculations, we can note some significant facts. In the early stages of her post-war recovery, Japan could draw on a large reserve of agricultural labour of low productivity, for whom a transfer into industry meant an immediate leap in the value of their output. The widespread belief that the conquest of foreign markets was achieved by low wages has long since ceased to be true, and Japanese wages have risen to European levels. The Japanese have a high saving rate, and the country's investment rate of around 30 per cent of GNP was well above the top European rates of around 20–24 per cent. Japan also has an excellent education system, a long tradition of regular government and a law-abiding population, and her government policy was focused actively and intelligently on achieving a high rate of growth of both output and exports. Yet when all these factors are taken into account, the nature of the market-oriented dynamic which drove the economy forward still remains something of a mystery.

Japan has more recently been joined by other highly successful economies on the rim of Asia. Leading among them were South Korea, Hong Kong, Singapore and Taiwan, the 'Eastern Tigers'. Apart from their economic vigour, they have little in common: two are city states, with trade as their main original occupation, the others have large territories with a substantial agrarian population which could be transferred to the modern sector; three were former colonies (which Hong Kong remained until 1997), whereas Taiwan was not; three had governments pursuing active growth policies,

Hong Kong had not. So far, however, they all have operated with low wages and poor social and working conditions for their labour, at low rates of social expenditure, and have been successful in generating varied bundles of export goods and services. At annual growth rates of 7 per cent or more, they are beginning to catch up on the leading western economies in terms of GNP per head. In 1993, the figures were, in terms of US dollars:

18,060 for Hong Kong,
19,850 for Singapore,
7,660 for South Korea, compared with
18,060 for the United Kingdom and
300 for India.

In terms of purchasing power parity, sometimes a better measure of real product, Hong Kong was at 87 per cent of the American figure, Singapore at 79 per cent, South Korea at 39 per cent, compared with the UK at 70 per cent.

Lately several other countries have registered steep growth curves, including Malaysia and Indonesia, both former colonies, and Thailand, which had never been subjected to colonial status by a European power. Since the early 1980s they have achieved growth rates of 7 per cent or over, in some cases exceeding 10 per cent a year, though in absolute terms they are still far behind the others.

THE THIRD WORLD

The oil states of the Middle East and North Africa form a category of their own. After the price rise and the increased imposts on the oil companies by the members of the OPEC cartel in 1973, the smaller countries among them had incomes which, averaged out per head, compared well with western European standards. However, it made relatively little difference to their populations, since most of the wealth remained in the hands of a small and now immensely wealthy ruling élite. Libya and Iran had policies to spread the wealth more widely, but the latter, together with Indonesia and Nigeria, was a populous country so that the effect on per capita income was less noticeable. Iraq wasted her oil riches in two costly wars of aggression, first against Iran (1980–8) and then by invading Kuwait (1990, driven out in 1991), which led ultimately to a world boycott of her oil and the drastic impoverishment of her people.

Most of the remaining, non-oil-exporting countries of the Third World did achieve considerable growth of output and incomes, yet proved unable to break through into prosperous modernity. The efforts by the international community in terms of direct aid and technical and economic advice had only modest success in the large majority of cases. A large number of countries is involved, and there are such huge differences among them that it is difficult to generalize. Two major groups may be discerned: countries which were at a modest level of per capita incomes, and those in absolute and dire poverty.

The most important group of countries among the former was made up of the Latin American republics, together with several of the Caribbean Islands. In terms of GNP per capita, they were, at the beginning of our period, well above the level of the really poor regions, averaging US $495 per head (at 1974 prices) in 1950, or three times as much as the figure for all developing countries, namely $160; in 1975 it was $944 compared with $375.[2] By 1993 this had reached $2,950 (at 1993 prices) compared with $300 for the low-income countries and $520 for Sub-Saharan Africa. Growth rates were therefore satisfactory: hovering around the very creditable annual rate for GNP of 5–6 per cent a year, they managed to produce per capita growth of up to 2–3 per cent in the face of the quite exceptional rate of population increase averaging no less than 2.9 per cent. Industrial production increased much faster than this, and several of the larger countries, in particular Brazil, the Argentine, Chile and Mexico, developed sizeable steel works, and some had car assembly plants, while Venezuela, Ecuador and Mexico, among others, produced large quantities of oil.

There were other favourable factors. The region possesses immense natural riches of minerals, forest products and fertile agricultural and grazing land. In most of the Latin American countries, half or more of the population was employed in agriculture at the beginning of our period compared with around 35 per cent at its end. Since productivity in industry was about four times that in the agrarian sector, the transfer of labour would have an immediate favourable effect on the economy. Further, the more developed countries in that region had a relatively high savings ratio of 16–20 per cent of GNP, boosted by capital imports of the order of 4 per cent of GNP,[3] and in the 1960s, at least, much United States aid was received. Yet, taking it all in all, economic progress has been considered to have been disappointing both by its own people and by outside observers. The disappointment lay partly in the political sphere, as most of the republics reverted from time to time to unstable and corrupt dictatorships – which may, indeed, by itself help to account at least partly for the failure to break through into economic modernity.

There were other causes for that failure. A major weakness is generally held to have been the economic dependence of the region. Dependent, usually for one or very few export commodities, on the markets of the advanced world, mainly the USA and Japan, the region did well in the war and immediate post-war years, when its export prices were high. But when these relative prices fell, the countries concerned turned to foreign loans to keep the boom going, and these soon became millstones round their necks, as described further in Chapter 6 below. The alternative policy of import substitution, that is, producing at home the manufactures which had hitherto been imported, foundered on the lack of technical expertise at all levels.

A second weakness was the very high rate of population increase. This led to a massive migration into the cities without diminishing the rural population: urbanization as measured by the World Bank increased from 57 per cent in 1970 to 71 per cent, among the highest in the world, in 1993. But since there was insufficient capital to employ the urban immigrants, they drifted into the shanty-towns, eking out a poverty-stricken marginal existence without adding much to national income. Third, the social and political structure, as it existed in many countries, kept power in the hands of land-owners and the army officer class associated with them, and offered little incentive and security to businessmen. Government policies caused, or failed to prevent, hyper-inflation and the collapse of the exchange value of the currency in several countries at the time of their debt crisis in the 1980s, the problem being aggravated by the tendency of the rich to send their capital abroad at such times. Lastly, most of these countries had failed to develop their infrastructure, and had made poor educational provision for the, mainly non-white, rural proletariat.

Yet by comparison with most of the rest of the Third World, Latin America was advanced and well off: it was highly urbanized, had a great deal of capital invested, and there was no question of large-scale famine, as there was in other parts of the non-industrialized world outside the communist orbit. There, much the largest economy was that of India. Unlike most other countries in its group, India had a relatively stable, functioning democratic government, a substantial well-educated élite and considerable industrial strength in absolute terms, though small in relation to the size of the population. Overall, however, India was still largely agricultural, some 72 per cent of the occupied population being engaged in agriculture in 1971 and, together with its neighbours, Bangladesh and Pakistan, it was among the poorest nations on earth.

Faced with the enormous task of modernization and industrialization, India's rulers on gaining independence determined to advance by steering the economy by a series of five-year plans beginning in 1951. The intention was not merely to create a wealthier, but also a juster society. About one-sixth of the country's investment went into agriculture, and some heavy industry was created; but much effort went to encouraging the processing industries for which India was well suited, such as working up flour, sugar, cotton or tobacco, and the small-scale 'smokeless' industries, many to be performed in the peasants' households, following Gandhi's philosophy. However, spread over a large population, the effects were minimal. Thus it has been calculated for 1971, that while North America consumed manufactured goods per head to the value of US $1,604 (at 1955 prices), western Europe of $950 and all non-industrial countries to the value of $49, the figure for India and Pakistan was a mere $16.[4] Starting from a very low level, much planning was faulty and bureaucratic, net savings were low, around 10 per cent of GNP, and despite the successful introduction of the 'green revolution' in 1967–8, there was a famine in 1972. India had to depend on some foreign investment and on foreign aid. She had been largely responsible for the formation of the International Development Agency (IDA) in 1960. Since she accepted some Russian aid, the USA were eager to help also, to prevent the country falling under Soviet influence.

In the end an industrial sector was established and there was growth, but in view of an annual population increase of 2.2 per cent, per capita incomes grew by only around 1 per cent a year over most of the period. In the 1980s, overall growth of GDP rose to an average of 6 per cent a year, but it fell back again in the early 1990s.

Several other countries, such as Ghana, also attempted to bridge the gap by a form of planning, but on the whole their success was no greater than that of the majority of the countries seeking to industrialize by means of market forces and foreign aid. There were mixed fortunes among them, but in general the poorest countries did worst: thus between 1950 and 1975, while all developing countries had between them an average annual growth rate in per capita GNP of 3.4 per cent, the low-income group among them, comprising in 1975 one-quarter of the world's population, grew by 1.1 per cent a year only.[5] In the 1980s, many of them, particularly in Sub-Saharan Africa, actually suffered an absolute decline in their per capita income, the average for the whole of Sub-Saharan Africa being *–1.1* per cent a year in 1984–93; some had even negative *total* growth in the early 1970s and again in the early 1980s, at a time when population was increasing. The worst years in that respect were 1981–3 and 1990–2. The 1980s have been described, with some justification, as the 'lost decade'. In that sense, the commonly adopted classification of these countries as 'developing' is something of a euphemism, though they all did show urban growth and an industrial and mining sector of some sort in existence at the end.

As far as natural resources were concerned, some of these countries, like Zaire, were richly endowed, while others were located in deserts or, like Bangladesh, were overcrowded in relation to their cultivable land. Virtually all had in common a lack of capital and of skilled manpower at all levels, with high rates of illiteracy in many cases. Virtually all also suffered from corrupt and incompetent, and often also undemocratic government. Aid from the advanced world in the form of capital goods, commodities and expertise had risen from US $7 billion in 1970 to $54.5 bn in 1993; Sub-Saharan Africa got $13.5 bn in 1990 and $16.4 bn in 1993, equivalent to 11.5 per cent of the region's GNP. However, apart from the medical assistance, which kept more people alive, the improvement which the aid managed to achieve was strictly limited.

THE CENTRALLY PLANNED ECONOMIES

The last group to be considered is made up of the centrally planned economies. At the beginning of our period, they would be counted among the developed countries, though among the poorest of them. The western group was dominated by the economy of the Soviet Union which had, as a result of the post-war settlement, pushed her borders far westward into Europe. Her allies or 'satellites' were disposed in a broad belt along that western border. Two of them, Czechoslovakia and East Germany, had substantial modern industrial sectors, others, including Hungary and Poland, had some more limited beginnings, while Bulgaria and Romania were largely agricultural. Yugoslavia and Albania soon dropped out of direct Russian control.

The Soviet Union managed to repair with extraordinary speed the bulk of the fearful ravages she had suffered and went on to show rapid progress until the late 1960s. Reliable statistics are hard to come by, in part because the official ones were doctored for political reasons, but partly also because the Soviets, unlike the western countries, included only goods and not services when calculating growth rates. There can be no doubt, however, that their economy made great strides while bearing an excessive armaments burden, and was quite capable of keeping pace in fields such as advanced nuclear technology and even taking the lead for a time in satellite construction. Growth, recalculated by American experts to western standards, averaged 4.8 per cent a year in the 1960s, falling to 2.4 per cent in the 1970s, to drop further to 2 per cent or less after 1980.

The other planned economies of eastern Europe had followed the Soviet line in nationalizing banking and all major industries, as well as (apart from Poland) collectivizing the bulk of their agriculture. They made equally remarkable progress, both in terms of building up a groundwork of industry and in showing rapid overall growth. Over large areas, backward peasant societies were being turned into urbanized manufacturing populations, an infrastructure of roads and means of communication was built up, illiteracy was banished and, not least, historic enemy nationalities learned to live together in peace. On the whole, the countries among them which had been most backward made the most rapid progress.

Yet, by the 1970s, it all went sour. There were several interconnected causes. Among the most important ones was the concentration on capital goods production, consumer goods being held back. This led to shortages and dissatisfaction at falling behind the known western standards of consumption, the grumbling, in turn, being contained by political repression. Full employment and faulty planning led to slackness of control and to mistakes in production. Unable to match the latest technology to emerge from the USA and Japan (as indeed was most of western Europe), these countries found, when attempting to import it, that their own exports were uncompetitive on world markets; in consequence, their purchases made them run into increasing debt to the west.

These and other economic causes were not the only ones to lead to a series of quiet revolutions from 1989 onward which toppled communist rule in the east, but they played an important part. Following these revolutions, planning was abolished and an aggressive market economy installed. The results, in the first years, were catastrophic, above all for the Soviet Union and her successor states, despite much western aid and the influx of western capital and entrepreneurship. Government finance for investment ceased and trading links between country and town, and between suppliers of raw materials and components and final goods manufacturers were broken, as were links between the republics which made themselves independent on the break-up of the USSR. Factories were closed, mass unemployment and runaway inflation followed, and the bottom dropped out of production. Even a number of transmissible killer diseases, which had virtually disappeared, returned to haunt these populations as vaccination and general hygienic measures were neglected. The 'economies in transition' as a group, as they are euphemistically called in United Nations statistics, saw their GNP *decline*:

in 1991 by –8.8 per cent,
in 1992 by –15.2 per cent,
in 1993 by –8.6 per cent and
in 1994 by –6 per cent.

By 1993, at purchasing power parity, the Russian GNP per head was no more than one-third of the American, and while the Czech republic was at 30.5 per cent, all the others were at 25 per cent or less, Romania having dropped to 11.3 per cent. The growth of decades was wiped out in a few years; and there is no end in sight. East Germany, the former German Democratic Republic, being incorporated into a unified Germany, suffered at once by coming into direct competition with an advanced economy, losing 40 per cent of jobs and half the output; but in the longer run, and with the aid of heavy subsidies paid by the western Länder (provinces), it has much the best chance of speedy recovery.

The fate of the eastern communist giant, China, was quite different. Early seeking independence from Soviet tutelage, as did her Marxist neighbours, North Korea and later Vietnam, she deliberately followed a different path to her socialist goal. In view of her bulk and variety, China may be considered to be a continent rather than a country; nevertheless, the Marxist government in power after 1949 managed to maintain a remarkably tight control over the economy in its drive to industrialization and then prosperity.

China's progress was marked by a number of stages or policy jumps, enforced, often with a great deal of brutality, by a disciplined Communist Party on the whole vast empire. In the early 1950s, local initiatives were fostered, and a 'hundred flowers' were encouraged to bloom. After a 'big push' in 1955–6 came a year of rest, followed by the 'great leap forward' of 1958–60. Both agriculture and industry were to advance, the latter helped by small village industry, including the famous backyard steel furnaces. There followed a crisis, a famine and the withdrawal of Russian technical aid in 1960–2. In the next phase, modernization of agriculture was driven forward and complete industrial plants ordered from the west: this phase culminated in the notorious 'cultural revolution' of 1966–9, which involved cutting most links with the outside world and destroyed ruthlessly many of the achievements up to then, together with the professionals responsible for them. After some years of recovery, a more measured pace of progress was then resumed.

Despite these upheavals, there was remarkable economic progress, though from an abysmal level. Thus the electricity generated rose from 4.3 billion kwh in 1949 to 19.3 billion in 1957 and to 282 billion in 1979; steel production increased from around 10 million tons in 1965 to 34.5 million tons in 1979 – still very low on a per capita basis, but in absolute terms around double the British output. Gross investment increased from 21.4 per cent of GNP in 1952 to 34.6 per cent by 1979.

Thereafter, aided by a certain amount of decentralization, the Chinese economy truly took off. Part of the secret was a radical reform of agriculture in 1978–9, when market incentives were provided by the 'contract responsibility' system for farmers. Small-scale localized manufacture also grew, creating 30 million new jobs between 1978 and 87. Foreign investment was encouraged and brought in much capital, especially from expatriate Chinese. It averaged US $233 million in 1978–82, but by 1990 had reached an annual figure of $3,437 million. Real GDP per capita rose by the very satisfactory rate of 4.9 per cent p.a. in 1974–83, and then joined the very fastest Eastern Tigers over the whole period 1984–93 with growth at the cumulative rate of 8.4 per cent. Nothing like this had been seen anywhere in the west, and the Indian economy, with which China had been comparable up to then, was left far behind. All this, it should be stressed, was still at a very low absolute level. GDP per head, at purchasing parity rates, even in 1993 was only $546 (in 1988 prices), compared with $918 for all developing countries and $652 for Africa. But China, it should be remembered, contains almost one-quarter of the world's population. Should growth at that rate or anything approaching it continue, it will shift the weight of the world economy even more heavily to the East, following the movement initiated by Japan and the Eastern Tigers.

To sum up. A major change in the production of the world's goods was the rise of the Far East, which appeared to be capable of absorbing the technology developed in the west together with the social changes to make it effective, with remarkably little friction. Elsewhere, those countries which were among the richest in the 1930s were still at the top in the 1990s, with some shifts among them, especially the *relative* decline of the USA and the UK. Their developed technical base and their traditional educational and value system, together with the favourable legal and political framework, gave them advantages which the rest of the world could not match quite so easily.

The middle-income countries grew fastest, except for the former planned economies which were severely disrupted by being turned into 'market economies' in the 1990s, but most had still a long way to go before catching up with the leaders. The very poorest mostly stayed poor, often because whatever limited output increase they could achieve was swallowed up by the increased number of people who had to be fed and supplied with capital.

5 Standards of living

THE DISTRIBUTION OF INCOMES

We have so far examined mainly changes in the quantities and mechanisms of production and productivity. None of these were ends in themselves: the ultimate object was to meet the requirements of consumers. This chapter will examine the changes in the world economy related to the provision of goods and services from the point of view of their consumers, generally summarized as changes in the standard of living.

In a purely numerical sense, the national product, in total and on a per capita basis, which has been at the centre of discussion up to now, is a good general indicator of the standard of living of a society or of the individuals in it. As output goes up so, broadly speaking, does consumption, at much the same rate. The standard of living enjoyed in a society with a high average GNP per head will be correspondingly better than that in a society with a low GNP per head. Conversely, the decline of output in eastern Europe after 1989 was reflected in the dire poverty of large numbers of people, especially in the cities. For the world as a whole, the successes of the producers in raising output since 1945 have borne fruit in the world's rising standard of living.

Moreover, in market-oriented societies, that is outside the planned economies, the way in which individuals distribute their expenditure in order to maximize their satisfaction, ultimately determines the decisions in the production sector, since producers want to sell what they have made. For example, as people become better off, the share of their incomes going on food (though not the absolute amounts) declines; that of luxuries increases. In consequence, world output of food will rise less fast, and become a smaller part of the total, as the world becomes richer. Against this, leisure goods, electronic equipment or motor car production will increase faster than total GNP, though both will also be influenced by relative price and cost changes.

Yet the broad correspondence between average income measured in money, and consumption does not fully account for standards of living. It has to be modified by several other considerations not directly to be read off from the income statistics. Real welfare, to the extent that it is linked to economic conditions, is exceedingly difficult to measure directly, and various proxy data which are measurable have been used in the past. These included the consumption of certain nutrients; the suicide rate; urbanization and its structure; ease of social mobility; and cultural facilities. Here we shall consider the following: the distribution of incomes; economic security; health and education; and environmental effects.

It may be taken for granted that the rich everywhere, even in the poorest countries, enjoy a reasonable standard of living. The test for a society would lie in how the average and how the poor live. Therefore, in order to translate average national income into human satisfaction, its distribution has to be taken into account. Moreover, while the absolute level of real income in a country matters, one's relative position also has an effect on one's sense of well-being: relative deprivation, doing worse than one's neighbours, may be felt as a disadvantage as much as, say, being poorly clad. It is thus with some justification that the European Union defines 'poverty' not in absolute terms, but as income at a level of less than half the average of the society.

It is not easy to measure the distribution of incomes even if the data are known, which has not often been the case in the past. Calculations based on incomes per family may yield different results for incomes per head according to whether or not we include the numbers per family in the calculations. Here we adopt a rough and ready indicator, used widely in modern times. We imagine all incomes, irrespective of numbers in families, lined up by size, from the lowest to the highest, and then measure the share of the total national income accruing to the lowest 20 per cent, and the highest 10 per cent of income receivers.

It is generally assumed that inequality widens in the early years of industrialization, to level out again later. Nowadays, some of the least equitable distributions are found in very poor Third World countries, such as Tanzania and Honduras, as shown in Figure 5.1.[1] By contrast, the planned economies of eastern Europe showed the most equitable distribution. In India, too, the political programme

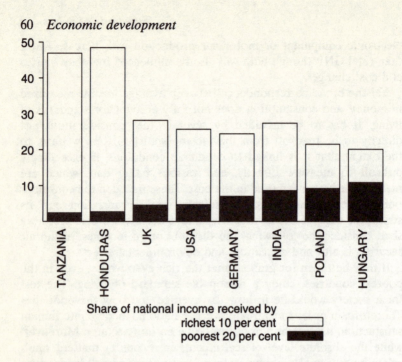

Figure 5.1 Income distribution in selected countries, *c.* 1990

had lessened inequality. The advanced industrial countries lay generally between the two extremes.

Not many comparable data exist for earlier years, but some information is available for various dates between 1975 and 1980. A comparison of those years with the more recent period shows that for poorer countries there was a move to greater equality, while among most of the industrialized countries there was a move to greater inequality. In India, for example, the gap between the richest 10 per cent and the poorest 20 per cent was reduced by –8.3 per cent of total incomes.

In Thailand, it increased by +0.7 per cent,
in Germany, by +1.3 per cent,
in the USA, by +2.3 per cent, and
in the UK, by no less than +6.7 per cent.

These movements were not unconnected with the widespread changes in economic policy which will be described in Chapter 8 below.

EMPLOYMENT AND UNEMPLOYMENT

An important aspect of the real standards of living is the security and regularity of the income received. Methods of payment vary enormously in the world today, but we may distinguish two main types of economic agents: those who are independent or self-employed, such as shopkeepers or peasant farmers, and those who receive a wage or salary. Both groups benefit from general boom conditions and suffer in depressions. Farmers producing cash crops for the market, especially in Third World countries, are particularly vulnerable to changes in world prices, in subsidies, taxes or tariffs, and these have hit them hard in recent years. For wage and salary earners, the unemployment statistics are good indicators of their security and their expectation of regular incomes.

The quality of the data on unemployment varies widely between different countries, though in the industrialized world efforts have been made to calculate them on similar principles. There, rates were very low in the first two decades of the peace, after the immediate effects of the war had been dealt with: in most advanced countries they stayed below 2 per cent, though they were slightly higher in the USA and in Italy, while Switzerland returned year after year a rate of 0.0 per cent.[2] At that level, all those who wanted to work could find jobs and could be certain that if one job was lost, another would soon be found. People out of work were mainly those unemployable for medical or other reasons, and those temporarily between jobs.

In the mid-1970s unemployment began to rise. Among the most powerful industrial economies, the 'Group of Seven', which included Japan with her low rates, average unemployment rose from 3.1 per cent in the 1960s to 4.6 per cent in the 1970s and to a peak of 7.0 per cent in 1994. Among the countries of the European Union it was 2.1 per cent in the 1960s, but had risen to an average of no less than 10.7 per cent by 1994. There were wide differences between countries, Spain, for example, recording a rate of well over 20 per cent, while Switzerland was still doing much better than average, as was Japan. As it became clear that unemployment at a high level would be by no means ephemeral, but would become a long-term burden on the economy, the expected cost of benefit payments led many countries to cut back on entitlements and to tighten definitions, so that the meaning of these statistics has begun to diverge once more. In 1993 there were, in the fourteen countries of western and northern Europe together with the USA, Canada, Australia and

New Zealand, no fewer than 28.9 million people registered as being out of work, and in 1994 the figure was virtually unchanged, at 28.8 million.

Unemployment became a major catastrophe in the lives of millions of families. In the new conditions of the labour market, those out of work could no longer expect to find new jobs easily. As firms shedding labour tried to shield their own staff from the worst effects of the cuts by placing the burden on new intakes, the young, looking for their first jobs, were disproportionally hard hit, as were older people, the unskilled and members of ethnic minorities. Unemployment rates within some of these special groups in certain locations reached 30 per cent, 40 per cent or even more, and for them, the hope of ever finding employment faded, with serious consequences for individual and social psychology. At the same time, the state of mind even of those in work was affected by the prevailing uncertainty and fear of redundancy.

The unemployment data relating to the less developed economies are much less reliable. Though some countries did show considerable unemployment even in the good years of the 1950s and 1960s, the Philippines, Syria, Argentina and Venezuela, for example, recording rates of 6 per cent or more, and Trinidad and Tobago upwards of 12 per cent,[3] these would often refer to the larger cities only, and omit part-time work or under-employment, rife in those economies. Moreover, since many city dwellers were recent immigrants, there was a tendency to return to the home village in times of stress, and disappear from the statistics. Peasant societies are notoriously prone to 'hidden unemployment' of people finding something to do on the farms, but not adding to the product which would not have been less, had they been absent.

Table 5.1, listing the 'open unemployment' which omits its hidden and part-time variants, shows that the developing economies may be classified into two groups. Some were clearly affected by the deterioration in economic life which had hit the advanced world from the 1970s onward. Those in the Far East, together with Mexico, changed in the opposite direction, the early 1990s being relatively good years.

HEALTH AND POPULATION

Eating habits and types of housing and its amenities differ widely and there is no satisfactory method of comparing them across frontiers. Some indirect evidence for the consequences of such conditions

Table 5.1 Open unemployment in some developing economies (in per cent)

	Early 1980s	Early 1990s
Egypt	5.2	10.6
Argentina	2.3	10.1
Bolivia	5.8	19.0
Trinidad and Tobago	10.0	19.8
Mexico*	4.2	3.8
China*	4.9	2.3
Republic of Korea	5.2	2.4
Singapore	3.0	2.6

* Some larger cities only
Source: United Nations, *World Economic and Social Survey 1994* p. 184

may be derived from comparing data on health, and in particular death rates and life expectation. Two facts stand out in relation to both of these. First, this period saw striking improvements in all regions of the globe. Second, the difference between rich and poor countries was, and remained, enormous.

In the advanced world rising incomes made it possible to improve public and private hygiene by better water supply and drainage, by more housing space, improved heating and ventilation, better nutrition, as well as by progress in medical science. Democratic pressure, added to the fear of epidemics which would not halt at the gates of the suburbs of the wealthy, led to various forms of universal or near-universal health insurance, so that no one needing medical attention went without. In the planned economies of eastern Europe and China these facilities were similarly made generally available in spite of their relatively low national income. In consequence of these and other improvements, life expectancy at birth in the developed economies, which averaged 56 years just before World War II, rose to 70 years in 1970 and 76 years by 1993: in Japan it had reached 80 years. This represents a quite astonishing improvement in barely two generations. In Latin America life expectancy rose even more dramatically from 40 years before the war to 60 years in 1970 and 69 years in 1993. China, in spite of her poverty, reached an average of 69 years in 1993 and India, 61 years. The remaining low-income countries improved their record from 30 years before the war to an average of 56 years in the same period.

Similar progress and similar divisions between rich and poor can be derived from death rates. Crude death rates which even in Europe would have approached 30 per 1,000 two centuries ago, had dropped in India to 19 in 1970 and 13 in 1993, in China to 16 and

10, scarcely different in the last year from those of the 'higher-income' countries, which averaged 10 and 9 per thousand in those years.

In these respects the mean, even for poor countries, was better than the best which the most privileged classes had been able to secure for themselves in the past. Most of this advance must clearly be attributed to progress in medical science which, partly through medical aid, benefited even the poorest regions. Individual treatment was backed by an understanding of what public actions were necessary, even though these were not always taken. The problems of the less developed countries are highlighted by the figures of the number of doctors. In the United Kingdom, for example, there was one physician for 810 people in 1970, with similar figures in Sweden (730), New Zealand (870) and even Poland (700). By contrast, in the low-income countries as a whole, excluding India and China, it was one for 20,640; for India the figure was 4,950, and for China, 1,500. By 1992 enormous strides had been made, but the ratio was still one doctor for 11,430 people in Zambia or one for 2,330 people in Honduras. In many countries, there was simply no skilled medical attention at all available in the countryside, apart from a handful of volunteers from the industrialized world.

People were not only living longer, they were healthier during their longer life span. Since 1945 a whole range of killer diseases has been conquered by antibiotics and other novel drugs. Other threats to life have been held in check by electronic scanners, sophisticated surgery, organ transplants, the use of lasers for treatment and a whole range of other methods not available to the pre-war world.

At the same time poor countries are still ravaged by diseases that have disappeared among the affluent. Infantile mortality rates, the deaths per 1,000 live births, a more sensitive indicator than crude death rates, show a frightening difference still between rich and poor as well as a steady improvement for both, as is illustrated in Figure 5.2.

Perhaps even more horrifying are the facts about malnutrition. In 1979–81, it was estimated that 494 million people were malnourished, or 23.6 per cent of the world population outside the industrialized regions. Averaging the years 1988–93, the percentage rates were 67 for Bangladesh, 63 for India, 47 for Ethiopia and 46 for Indonesia. Refugees were particularly likely to suffer from undernourishment: in 1991 there were about 20 million people in the world uprooted by conflicts, while 27 million Africans were

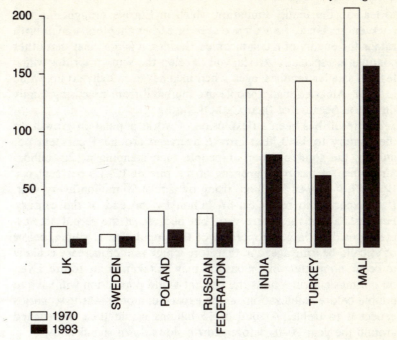

Figure 5.2 Infantile mortality in selected countries per thousand, 1970 and 1993

suffering from drought and required outside assistance to survive.[4] In their case there can clearly be no complacency over rates of progress.

Most of the poorer countries have high birth rates of around 40 per 1,000. In the past, these were matched by high death rates, so that population change, up or down, was held within narrow bounds. In Europe, when the death rate began to fall in the nineteenth century, there was a short phase of rapid population increase, but it was soon followed by a parallel fall in the birth rate – the 'demographic transition' – so that the overall population increase was kept relatively low once more.

The reasons for the falling birth rate are complex, but are related to the rising standards of living and social and personal priorities at the time. Among today's developing countries, these relationships are out of line with each other. Owing to medical advance, death rates are falling so fast that it is the resulting rapid population increase itself which prevents the kind of rising prosperity that used to lead to the family limitation which in Europe brought the two back into balance. As we have seen in earlier chapters, a high birth rate is the enemy of rising incomes. Besides, it is not clear that other continents, especially Africa, will develop the same priorities which lead to smaller families, even when incomes eventually go up, while in Latin America many people are inhibited from practising family limitation because of their Catholic faith.

The result has been an explosion of world population growth. In the century to 1940, that growth averaged around 1 per cent per annum, the total number of people then standing at 2.3 billion. Since then, it has been growing at the rate of 1.7–1.8 per cent p.a. By 1987, it topped 5 billion, rising by almost 90 million every year. It is expected to reach 6¼–6½ billion by the end of the century. Forecasts about the future vary, but because of the recent accelerated growth, a large proportion of the population is young, below or at child-bearing age, and therefore a high rate of increase is likely to occur, no matter what measures may be taken in the future. Even on optimistic assumptions the present world population will have to double before stabilization can be expected; more realistic scenarios expect it to treble. A total of 15 billions would then be reached around the year 2040, before growth slows down significantly.[5]

The problems posed by such growth are aggravated by the fact that most of it occurs in the poorer countries. The high-income countries had birth rates of 17 per 1,000 in 1970 with death rates at 10, a gap, or growth, of 7 per 1,000, or 0.7 per cent a year; by 1993 this had narrowed to 13 and 9, a gap of 4. China, which had made great efforts to halt the rise in numbers by attempting to enforce a limit of one child per family, still had rates of 39:16, or a gap of 23 (that is, a growth of 2.3 per cent a year) in 1970, reduced only slightly, to 29:10, a gap of 19, in 1993. Most of the developing countries of southern Asia and Africa, as well as much of Latin America, had net growth rates between 2 and 3 per cent a year, Africa very close to 3 per cent. Moreover, there is in all these regions a rapid rise in urbanization, at rates of 4 to 6 per cent a year, which will tend to increase pauperization still further until such times as industrial or commercial employment can be found for these impoverished and unskilled migrants. According to United Nations estimates, half the world's population will be urban by the end of the century, and eighteen of the twenty-one largest cities will by then be in the developing countries.

EDUCATION

One mechanism which may speed the move to a demographic transition, and which at the same time is also an important indicator of standards of living, is the improvement of educational provision. There has been a true revolution in this field since the war, even in the industrialized countries. These started with virtual universal provision for elementary education, widespread attendance at secondary education, and an élite tertiary, or university system. An enormous expansion then occurred in the secondary sector and was accompanied by rises in the school-leaving age. For universities, the growth was breathtaking, averaging around 9 per cent a year in the 1960s and 5 per cent in the 1970s. As Table 5.2 shows, excluding the United States which had started with much higher numbers, students in all institutions of higher education increased eightfold to the mid-1970s. Growth has slowed since then, in part because so many of that age group were in institutes of higher education already. Education of this kind has to be seen as a consumer good as well as a capital investment. Young people are given a chance to savour the achievements of their civilization and lead a fuller life; at the same time, they are being prepared for the complex and skilled jobs which the modern economy demands from a growing proportion of the work force.

In the Third World, progress varied; it was fast in some countries, but even by the end of our period did not compare with the richer communities because of the low starting level. Taking as our measure the proportion of the age groups for whom secondary education is provided, usually those between 10 and 18, or 11 and 18 years of age, who are actually at school, this had reached 73 per cent in the United Kingdom in 1970, rising to 86 per cent in 1992; in Sweden it was higher still, at 86 and 91 per cent respectively. The countries with Marxist governments once again did better than their national income level would have warranted, spending a high proportion of their GNP on education: thus Poland was at 62 and 83 per cent, only marginally below the rich western European level, and China was at 24 and 51 per cent, far above the other countries in her income range. Here, too, the upward trend was notable.

Against this, in the developing world the ratios were 26 and 44 per cent in India, 14 and 38 per cent in Ghana and a mere 3 and 5 per cent in Tanzania. It may be doubted if the quality, either, compared with that available in Europe, North America or Japan. Higher education there, as Table 5.2 shows, has rapidly expanded

Table 5.2 Students in institutes of higher education (in thousands)

	c. 1950	*c.* 1975	*c.* 1990
Developed economies			
Canada	69	888	1,943
USA	2,659	12,097	14,361
Japan	391	2,249	2,887
Belgium	20	160	271
France	138	1,076	1,840
Germany (West)	90	1,041	1,799
Italy	146	1,118	1,533
Netherlands	28	288	479
Spain	50	540	1,169
United Kingdom	105	733	1,258
Australia	31	324	536
Totals	3,727	20,514	28,076
Totals without USA	1,068	8,417	13,715
Developing economies			
Algeria		42	286
Egypt		480	708
Kenya		6	35
Libya		13	73
Morocco		45	221
Mexico		562	1,311
Argentina		597	1,077
Totals		1,745	3,711

Source: *Statistical Yearbook of the United Nations*, Annual

in recent years, though there was a strong tendency among students to go for subjects such as law and politics which had a high prestige because they led to occupations traditionally held by the ruling classes and did not involve 'dirtying one's hands', rather than the technical and biological subjects desperately needed by these societies. Nor had the backlog of more elementary education been made up. Thus as recently as 1990, India was believed to have an adult illiteracy rate of 66 per cent, Sub-Saharan Africa 62 per cent and low-income countries as a whole (excluding India and China), some 49 per cent. In Latin America it ranged from 7–20 per cent. In the industrialized world it has long since become a negligible quantity.

ENVIRONMENTAL DAMAGE

Not all effects of economic growth on standards of living were positive. Among the most far-reaching adverse factors was the damage to the environment, brought about directly by higher incomes, as well as by increased numbers of people. Some of this, at the individual level, is well-known: the noise and air pollution of the cities, including the notorious smog of Los Angeles, Tokyo or the Ruhr region, the traffic jams and the many thousands of lives lost every year in road accidents, and the crowded and polluted beaches all around the European coastline. But the threats to human standards of comfort, even of survival, were considerably more far-reaching.

Among the best known were the inroads into the ozone layer caused by the use of aerosols of chlorofluorocarbons (CFC). Large holes have been discovered, in particular over the Antarctic region, and even if no further damage occurs (and some of the less developed countries have not yet enforced an end to the pollution) it will be a hundred years before the original protective layer is restored. Another threat at global level is the so-called 'greenhouse effect' of warming caused by excessive carbon dioxide in the atmosphere. It has come about in part by the greatly extended burning of fossil fuel, while at the same time large parts of the forests which performed the necessary photosynthesis have been cut down. Since the eighteenth century the proportion of carbon dioxide in the air has gone up by one-quarter, from 280 to 350 parts per million. No one can estimate the long-term effects of this pervasive change, but it has been noticed that the ice cap of the poles is beginning to melt, and glaciers have shrunk by a measurable extent.

Another widespread source of pollution has been the use of nitrogenous and other fertilizers as well as chemical pesticides on the land. Many of these substances are gradually washed down rivers and into lakes and oceans. There they often join chemicals, and especially heavy metals, disposed of by chemical firms and others. An excess of nitrogen causes eutrophication of the water: as the oxygen disappears, algae cover the waters and fish life ceases. Lakes in Canada and the Soviet Union provide well-known instances. In other areas poisoned fish enter the human food chain and cause illness and death among the human population, as has happened in Japan.

Carbon dioxide, above all from car exhausts, and heavy metals in the atmosphere also, damage the forests and other plants: in some of the more heavily populated parts of Europe, half or more of the trees are affected. 'Acid rain' of acidic sulphur oxides is a consequence of modern high consumption. The dangers of DDT, a powerful insecticide, were recognized early on, and its use generally prohibited by the early 1970s, but the reactions to other dangerous substances have been slower. One problem which has arisen towards the end of our period was the tendency of micro-organisms to develop strains immune to the antibiotics that have done so much to reduce the incidence of disease and death. The lethal effects of asbestos were not discovered until thousands of workers were poisoned, as well as those living in dwellings, and working in factories and schools in the building of which the substance had been incorporated. The causes of silicosis and pneumoconiosis among miners, grinders and others, however, had been recognized earlier and their incidence reduced before World War II.

The regulation and damming of flowing water have brought dangers of their own. Thus, to take some well-known examples, the Moselle-Rhine system is more liable to repeated flooding than before, while the great Assuan Nile dam affected the scouring powers of the water and led to the pollution of the Mediterranean around the river delta. Large-scale drainage and irrigation works have almost emptied the Aral Sea in the former Soviet Union, which may be considered a major environmental catastrophe in itself.

Other catastrophes have been associated with chemical works. The emission of TCDD from the Seveso plant in Italy in July 1976, which poisoned a large area was an early well-known example, but it was put entirely in the shade by the accident to the Union Carbide plant in Bhopal, India, in December 1984. There about 2,250 people died and 200,000 others were injured, many of them blinded, when the insecticide methyl-isocyanide escaped into the atmosphere.

Even greater, and more lasting, damage was done by the explosion of one of the nuclear plants at Chernobyl in the Soviet Union in April 1986. Apart from the immediate deaths, a large part of the Ukraine suffered long-term poisoning, and the incidence of illness and physical defects among the victims and their children is by no means over, nor is it certain that the wrecked power unit itself has been safely encased. Nuclear power, hailed earlier on as a non-polluting source of energy since there was no carbon dioxide emission, has turned out to be potentially more dangerous than anything that mankind has created before. There were numerous smaller accidents before Chernobyl, including one at Chelyabinsk in 1958 in which land in a radius of 200 km became radioactive, and there is now a new source of danger from discarded nuclear waste. Anxiety particularly arises from the decommissioned Russian nuclear submarines likely to pollute the Arctic sea because of leakage of their metal containers. Another cause of concern is the practice of moving nuclear waste for disposal to developing countries, to the West Coast of Africa from Europe, and to Latin America from the USA, where poverty induces governments to accept the risks without being fully in command of a safe technology.

In the past, there has been a broad tendency for countries in the early stages of industrialization to neglect the protection of their citizens from environmental damage, but as wealth and technical know-how increase, together with the democratic power of those most affected, counter-measures are taken. In Europe and the USA governments began from the mid-nineteenth century onward to prohibit the emission of noxious fumes or substances in towns, the pollution of drinking water or the working of unfenced machinery. Modern dangers have led to modern equivalents: Britain has had a Clean Air Act since 1956, the USA a Water Quality Act, and most advanced countries enforce catalysers in new cars and maintain extensive recycling schemes. Typically, they now spend 1–1.5 per cent of their GNP to prevent pollution, the figure for Japan being as high as 2 per cent.

The larger environmental problems necessarily need international agreements, which by their nature are difficult to achieve and even more difficult to enforce. The Conference on Desertification had virtually no practical results. However, the Montreal Protocol of 1987 has been quite effective, at least among the developed countries, to reduce CFC emissions, and the United Nations Conference on Environment and Development which took place in Rio de Janeiro in June 1992, described as the largest gathering of world leaders ever held, agreed to two conventions, one on Biological Diversity, to protect species, and the other on Climatic Change, to reduce carbon dioxide emission. These were signed by 153 states, and a Global Environmental Facility (GEF) was set up to provide funds for the poorer countries to carry these decisions into effect. Even if most governments continue to drag their feet, official world opinion is important, and was supported in Rio by a parallel Global Forum at which 2,000 non-governmental organizations were represented.

At one time it used to be thought that the countries with a planned economy would escape the harmful tendency of private firms in market economies to endanger the environment in the search for profit, because they were not responsible for meeting the cost of the consequences. There, it was assumed, it would be the same agency, the state, which was both controlling the factories and having to meet the costs of pollution. It turned out that these hopes were misplaced, and these countries came to be among the worst offenders. This was so in part because detailed planning was split among many departments without responsibility for each other's actions, in part because they were always subject to a strong drive to show short-term successes, and in part because these societies lacked democratic methods which would permit the victims to influence the course of events. The Soviet disasters of Chernobyl, the Aral Sea and the leaking submarines have been mentioned already. Another major catastrophe was the poisoning of the huge Lake Baikal by the discharge of two cellulose plants: a widespread agitation in the early 1970s, and a Soviet Council on Environmental Problems, established in 1973, remained powerless to prevent this, since the factories were working for the military.

Leaving the Soviet Union aside, Poland and East Germany became the most unrestrained polluters in Europe. Cracow, an ancient city some forty miles to the east of the heavy industry of Nova Huta, was among the main sufferers. Owing to its poisoned air, its people had double the rate of lung cancer, and a life expectation 3–4 years less than the rest of Poland. The oxygen content of the air had dropped from 21 per cent to 17 per cent. Elsewhere, factories had no water purification plants and the poisons rolled down the rivers into the bay of Gdansk. As a result, the oxygen content there had dropped to 0 per cent in many places, poisonous substances exceeded the permitted level by a factor of 100, and no seals, pike, plaice or eels had survived. According to the Polish Minister for the Environment, in 1988 the damage done to the country by pollution was of the order of 1 billion zloty, or 10–15 per cent of GNP.

The subject of environmental damage is a wide one, and only a small number of representative examples could be given here. But two general remarks may be made. The first is that this is an area in which the calculations of private profit, which provide the mainspring of market economies, are inadequate, since private costs diverge substantially from social costs or benefits. Our age has found that an overriding political authority, be it a national or local government, has to have powers of intervention and restraint on the self-seeking policies of private business in order that genuinely rational decisions may be made in the light of all the consequences.

Second, the examples provided make it clear that true standards of living, including the quality of life, are not to be measured by real incomes alone. A measure for the diseconomies, the costs and the burdens which do not appear in the usual balance sheets is required. Some economists, such as Nordhaus and Tobin[6] have thought to provide a more broadly based 'measure of economic welfare' (MEW), in which negative quantities, including environmental losses, are deducted from the crude real income figures. It will hardly be doubted that, even taking these into account, our age still saw a considerable rise in real standards of living, but it will not be as large as the widely used monetary figures would have us believe.

Part II
Economic policy

6 Global economic policies

IMF AND WORLD BANK

Towards the end of World War II, when victory for the Allies seemed assured, discussions began to determine the shape of the post-war world, which the victorious powers were able to influence to a very large extent. Within the political-diplomatic sphere, which falls outside the boundaries of this volume, the United Nations was founded to replace the practically defunct League of Nations. As far as the world economy was concerned, a number of key decisions were taken at a conference of delegates of forty-four nations held at Bretton Woods in New Hampshire in July 1944.

It was a time when the United States held virtually all the levers of economic power in her hands, and the structures which evolved were essentially those proposed by the American representatives. Two major institutions were created as a result of Bretton Woods: the International Monetary Fund (IMF) and the Bank for International Reconstruction and Development, commonly known as the World Bank. In due course most countries took up membership: thus the IMF had 179 members by 1994 and the Bank had 177. Their founders were strongly influenced by the lessons drawn from the inter-war years and were determined not to repeat the mistakes which had led then to world depression and war.

It had been the experience of the 1930s that countries suffering from unemployment were likely to try to improve their position by devaluing their currencies. By this means their exports would appear cheaper to foreign buyers, who would therefore buy more of them, while at the same time foreign imports would be cut because they would now appear dearer. In that way they hoped to create more jobs at home. Some countries imposed even cruder methods, for example controlling and rationing foreign currencies or obstructing imports in order to stop their people buying things from abroad. The trouble was that other countries could retaliate by doing the same, and there ensued an ever-widening campaign of devaluations and obstructions to trade and payments which disrupted commerce and harmed everyone. The IMF was designed to prevent a recurrence of that sequence of events.

One of its basic ideas was that in order to prevent that kind of competitive devaluation which had been so harmful in the 1930s, exchange rates of all currencies would be fixed right at the start and not changed thereafter, except in defined special circumstances. Since the most likely threat to a fixed exchange rate system was presumed to be a payments imbalance, that is, a country being unable to pay for its imports with sufficient exports, the IMF was designed to be a holder of a buffer stock of currencies, ready to tide members over such difficult years.

The system was to work in the following way. Each member country would, usually through its Central Bank, pay a deposit into the Fund, mainly in its own currency but to the extent of one-quarter in gold or dollars. The size of the in-payment was determined on a quota basis calculated to be roughly in proportion to a country's economic strength. If it got into difficulties, in the sense of owing to other member countries more than it could pay by exports, the Fund would lend it the required sum out of its stock of currencies held. That loan had to be repaid within five years. However, the larger the required loan, the more stringent the conditions and there was a maximum, thus discouraging heavy borrowing. The penalties on excessive borrowers were, however, not matched by comparable penalties on excessive lenders: it was obvious at the time that the lender whose currency would be in greater demand than any other would be the United States. The only defence against the excessive lender was that its currency could be declared a 'scarce currency', and then other countries could impose certain restrictions on imports from that country.

Clearly, this was a structure designed to deal with short-term problems, and if the payments deficit of a country was indeed due to some temporary blip, the IMF could help. But if, as was commonly the case, it was due to a more persistent structural weakness, the country concerned was expected to use the loan in order to undertake remedial action. Three types of possible action had been known in the inter-war years: a country might devalue its currency – but that was precisely what was prohibited under the IMF rules; it could raise tariffs or in other ways hamper imports – but that, as we shall see, would break other international agreements, and in any case the IMF was specifically intended to secure freedom of trade; or, third, it could go in for policies of internal deflation, that is, it could take steps to reduce the incomes of its people, so that less was available to be spent on imports. However, such policies, which involved unemployment, would be unpopular, would damage the economy and, in contrast to the inter-war years, had become politically unacceptable.

In practice, therefore, even in the period up to 1971 during which the gold-dollar base held up and the system worked reasonably well, countries with serious and persistent balance of payments difficulties opted for devaluation, with or without consent of the IMF. Thus in 1949 sterling was devalued by 31 per cent and a large number of countries followed suit; other countries, including Germany, the Netherlands and Switzerland, revalued (that is, up-valued) their currencies at different times in those years.

In 1971 there was a drastic change. The dollar, hitherto thought to be as good as gold itself, came off the gold standard, and at the same time the regime of fixed exchange rates came to an end. Currencies were allowed to 'float' and they did so in different ways, though there were various regional schemes to peg some currencies to each other, as we shall see in the next chapter. This represented a critical break in world economic policy: it meant, in effect, the end of an era based on the post-war settlement. The original task of the IMF to ensure that exchange rates remained fixed had ended in failure.

By contrast, the IMF's role as a provider of an international currency reserve had expanded far beyond the initial concept. Even before 1971, it had ceased to be simply a supplier of dollars and had begun to meet much more varied needs. For one thing, other currencies were now in demand. Thus, in the four years 1967–70, dollar drawings totalled $2,850 million, while those in other currencies came to no less than $6,247 million. Beyond this, the initial deposits soon proved inadequate to the task of providing a significant share of the world's liquidity as trade grew and the value of the dollar fell. There followed a series of substantial, almost spectacular increases in the loanable funds handled by the IMF. The quotas were raised in 1959, again in 1965 (for some) and once more in 1970, increasing the available funds from US $9.3 billion to almost $29 billion in the process. Meanwhile, in 1962, the ten largest countries concluded the General Agreement to Borrow (GAB) to lend the Fund up to $10 billion, and in 1966–7 the Group of Ten devised an entirely new access plan of resources for borrowers in the form of Special Drawing Rights (SDRs), to be provided by members but drawn through the IMF. In 1970–2 $9.5 billion were set aside, and another $12 billion in 1979–81, though meanwhile other forms of liquidity had been developed. Although the gold base had hardly changed in the interim, the sums that could be counted as international reserves had rather spectacularly increased tenfold from $47.4 billion in 1945 to $477.7 billion in 1985.[1]

By then the main function of the IMF had changed once more. It had now become a reserve holder for the developing world: by 1980–1, 93 per cent of its credits went to it. These countries had special needs, and were likely to suffer more severely from the decline of certain commodity prices as well as from external shocks. As early as 1963, the Compensatory Financial Facility (CFF) was authorized to provide credit to offset falls in their export earnings. This was extended in 1976 to help in case of excessive wheat import costs and in 1990 for the same purpose for oil imports. An Oil Facility had been set up in 1974 to meet the first price increase, and a Supplementary Financing Facility (SFF) in 1979.

However, the developing countries were not only from time to time desperately in need of credit; they were also less able to repay their loans than the industrialized nations for whom the IMF had initially been planned, and many dragged out their loans far beyond the regulation five years, turning the IMF against its will into a provider of long-term credit. More drastic measures had to be taken to protect the IMF's funds. It developed the principle of 'conditionality', which meant inspecting the borrowing country from time to time to make sure the funds were 'properly' applied. Countries were expected to use the IMF's funds in line with its own notions of what constituted good housekeeping to ensure repayment and this, in turn, caused resentment among the recipients. As mainly an issuer of loans to the poorer nations, the IMF had by the 1980s inevitably become involved in the global debt problem of that decade, to be discussed further below.

The World Bank, the other institution devised at Bretton Woods, was from the start intended to provide long-term loans. Its structure differed basically from the IMF in possessing only limited resources of its own – the initial capital being US $10 billion, of which only 20 per cent were paid up – acting instead as an intermediary between borrowing countries and providers of credit. Such credit would be raised in the market by issuing bonds, repayable in the same currency. The Bank was limited to development projects which promised reasonable returns, but which for one reason or another were unable to attract private funds directly.

In its early years, its loans went mostly to war-devastated European countries; in the 1950s they tended to be switched to middle-income countries and others inhabited by Europeans overseas; and thereafter they went almost exclusively to developing economies. These had received 47 per cent of the loans in 1948–52, but accounted for well above 90 per cent from 1970 onwards. The key was to help them on to a development path, while also, about that time, under the influence of its chief executive, Robert S. McNamara, the Bank set itself the task of lessening poverty in the world.

There was much optimism in the first two decades of its working: given reasonable projects and technical advice, it was believed, the loans for capital investment made available through the World Bank would soon lead to structural transformation which would allow sustained growth into economic development to take place. At the same time the creditors, such as American and western European banks, insisted on generally 'sound' overall economic policies on the part of the receiving governments, in particular policies which favoured market orientation and *laissez-faire*.

These obligations were enforced much more strictly in the deteriorating world economic conditions from the 1970s onward, in which commodity prices collapsed with devastating effects on some Third World countries. Denationalization, deregulation and liberalization of markets, and measures to benefit enterprise and weaken trade unions, became almost routine. Budget deficits were to be met by tough deflationary measures, which caused widespread unemployment and much hardship among many of the weaker economies.

Yet at the same time, banks often tended almost to force their loans on to the poorer countries, sometimes known as the 'South': the reason was the declining investment opportunities in the richer 'North'. New types of 'softer' loans, carrying easier conditions, were introduced under the aegis of the International Development Association (IDA) and the International Fund for Agricultural Development. An International Finance Corporation (IFC) was set up to promote the private sectors in the poorer nations and the Multilateral Investment Guarantee Agency (MIGA), founded in 1988, was to protect foreign direct investors there. World Bank lending was targeted either on 'structural adjustment' (SAL) or the more specific 'sectoral adjustment' (SECAL).

Commitments of the World Bank rose from (current) US $610 million in 1961 to $1,680 million in 1970 and $14,244 million in 1994.

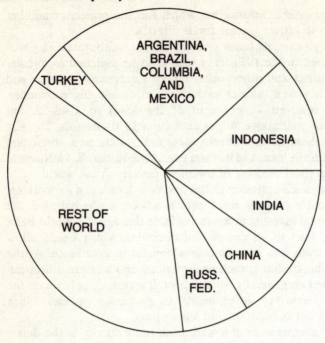

Figure 6.1 Shares of the $109.3 billion of World Bank loans outstanding in 1994

The major recipients of the total of $109.3 billion of loans outstanding in 1994, are shown in Figure 6.1. Other countries which received $2 billion each or more were South Korea, Morocco, Nigeria, Pakistan, the Philippines and Hungary.

PROBLEMS OF THE THIRD WORLD

The World Bank also provided a small element of aid, but basically its task lay in mediating straightforward loans. Although enquiries by the Bank's staff which preceded these loans were becoming highly intrusive, their general goodwill for benefiting the populations of Third World countries could not be doubted. Nevertheless, the governments of most of the developing countries were dissatisfied, alleging that the international organizations like the World Bank were acting in the interest of the creditor countries, above all the USA, rather than in their own. They demanded more comprehensive measures to promote self-help through changes, particularly in commercial policy, rather than aid with strings attached and, enjoying a majority of the voting power at the United Nations, they were not without political influence. At a meeting in Geneva in 1964 they created a permanent organization for themselves, the United Nations Conference on Trade and Development (UNCTAD) to press their demands.

At the UNCTAD meeting in Algiers in 1967, the 'Group of 77' of the so-called non-aligned states – there would ultimately be over 100 of them – devised a Charter which in 1974 became the 'Charter of Economic Rights and Duties of States'. The rights were to be theirs; the duties were to be those of the industrialized countries. These were to include, beside loans and grants for the Third World, preference for their manufactured exports and favourable prices for the primary goods imported from them, plus subsidies if world prices moved against the developing countries and for other purposes. Further, they wanted international monetary reform in their interest, the regulation of transnational companies, and regularized transfer of technology from the advanced nations to themselves. Altogether, the so-called Lima Declaration demanded that their share of world manufacturing should be raised from the current 8 per cent to 25 per cent.

The industrialized countries were not unwilling to make concessions, accepting the principles of the so-called New International Economic Order devised in 1973 and agreeing, again in principle, to set aside 1 per cent of their GNP for aid to the Third World, but were put off by the aggressive rhetoric and confrontational tactics of UNCTAD. It was clear that every proposal, whatever its exact form or context, amounted in the end to a transfer of resources from themselves to the developing countries, for which nothing was offered in return. Moreover, not all the poorer countries favoured all of these demands, since some would have lost out by them. It was thus not entirely surprising that the practical results of all that agitation turned out to be meagre. By 1979, when UNCTAD had adopted a more co-operative stance, an agreement on supporting staple prices was reached. Wide-ranging privileges were also granted by member states of the European Community to their former colonies, to be noted further in Chapter 7.

Meanwhile international aid, particularly to the poorest countries, was proceeding in numerous ways. Much of it was provided by non-governmental organizations, such as Oxfam, the Red Cross or Médecins sans Frontières; individual doctors, teachers and other specialists went out to work in these countries for a number of years. At times of crisis, such as the Ethiopian famines, additional funds would flow from public collections for relief. It was estimated in 1985 that there were some 2,000 non-governmental agencies in the OECD countries which were channelling private financial and human resources to development activities in 110 countries at a total cost of $2.4 billion, supplemented by $1 billion of government funds.[2] According to OECD data, official development finance commitments from all sources had risen from $59.5 billion in 1984 to $101.6 billion in 1991. The United Nations had started their own development programme (UNDP) in 1965.

Official aid and development assistance raised a number of complex issues. It was a new departure for which there was no historical precedent, except perhaps in the form of aid by a mother country for its colonies. Its very existence on such a broad base tells us something about the mood of the post-war world, for which again there was no precedent. It rested largely on a background feeling that those better off ought to help the poor, especially in the good years of the 1950s and 1960s, when the transfer of part of the year's growth would hardly be felt. But there was also the more mercenary thought that better-off countries make better trading partners and are less likely to turn to communism.

Yet there was also increasing criticism of these aid transfers as time went on, partly on the grounds that much of the aid that was sent out ended up in the pockets of members of corrupt governments and merely helped to keep tyrants in power, or, worse still, was used directly or indirectly by them to acquire arms to oppress their own people or attack a neighbour. Moreover, the spokesmen of the élites in control who raised the loudest clamour for aid, were frequently themselves well off, possibly by having exploited their own people, yet made no attempt to distribute on their part their own wealth among the poor.

Leaving simple grants aside, development assistance took various forms. In real terms it had risen by 67 per cent between 1970 and 1983, when it amounted to $36 billion, of which the industrialized market economies provided 76 per cent, the OPEC countries 15 per cent and the USSR and eastern Europe 9 per cent. By 1993, development assistance, this time from OECD and OPEC alone, had reached $54.5 billion. As a proportion of the GNP of the donor nations, it had remained unchanged at one-third of 1 per cent between 1970 and 1990, and then dropped to 0.30 of 1 per cent by 1993. The proportion varied greatly between countries, the Scandinavians and others among the smaller countries of Europe heading the list. The USA, always the leading donor in absolute terms, was steadily reducing her share over this period. In terms of the receiving countries, much the largest contribution was made to the nations of Sub-Saharan Africa: in 1993, development assistance, as noted in Chapter 4 above, amounting to 11.5 per cent of their GNP, again with considerable differences between individual countries.

THE WORLD DEBT CRISIS

To the extent that the funds which reached the Third World were in the form of loans, they had to be repaid in due course in addition to the interest payments which were payable, usually from the start. Different agencies, including local authorities or public corporations might be responsible for these reverse payments, but in the end it was the economy as a whole which had to earn a current surplus in foreign currency to meet those obligations to the foreign creditors. Where the loans were well used and conditions in world markets were favourable, the production derived from the capital investment created by the original loans should have provided that surplus, and something over. Where the investment was less soundly based, or the money had been used wastefully, no such surplus arose and the country was faced with the need to find foreign currency to service the loan, on top of its original difficulties. In practice, most countries emerged with a mixture of good as well as misplaced investments.

Whatever the details, it was in the nature of things that sooner or later, unless there was to be a never-ending, ever-increasing stream of loans from abroad, the outflow to service the borrowed capital, including interest and repayments, would exceed the incoming stream of foreign investment to the borrowing country. There was here a time-bomb waiting to explode as the total outstanding external debt of the developing countries increased inexorably from $636 billion in 1980 to $1,017 billion in 1985, to jump further, after a brief halt, to $1,601 billion in 1993. Various factors additional to the capital and loan service movements affect the external payments balance of countries but, as Table 6.1 shows, for the Third World as a whole, outflows were beginning to exceed the inflows in the 1980s.

It will be seen from the first two lines in the Table that the outgoing stream, still below the inward flow in 1982, was exceeding it by 1993. The next two lines refer to the rising direct investments by foreigners, usually by the multinationals, by which a negative balance in the earlier year was turned positive for the time being.

Table 6.1 Credit transfers of developing countries, 1982–1993 (US $ billion)

	1982	1993
Credits obtained	74.1	47.2
less interest, etc., paid back	−45.5	−52.3
Direct investments	7.2	37.9
less dividends, etc.	−9.3	−10.9
Net short-term borrowings	−29.9*	42.9
Grants	11.0	25.8
Total net transfers	7.1	90.6

* i.e. repayments
Source: United Nations, *World Economic Survey 1994*

Short-term movements fluctuated widely, while the last item, grants, refers to outright gifts in aid. The total, it will be noted, was positive in both years; however, it had been negative every year between 1983 and 1989, and had become positive once more only in 1990.

While this time-bomb was ticking away quietly, several factors combined to bring about the explosion in 1982, the world debt crisis year. Some of these go back to the oil price increases of 1973 and 1979. These had transferred billions of 'petrodollars' into the hands of oil-producing countries which lacked adequate investment opportunities at home. As noted above, they were therefore almost forcing their loans on to others, particularly on middle-income countries such as those of Latin America. At the same time, developing countries, faced with prices of oil and other imports which were rising faster than their export prices – their terms of trade deteriorated by 23 per cent between 1980 and 1985 – were only too eager to absorb foreign loans to bridge the gap. This could go on merrily for a time, but then interest rates began to rise, causing serious strain on the annual payments stream. The share of the export earnings which had to be diverted to service the debt for all developing countries together rose from 16 per cent in 1977 to 25 per cent in 1982, which in turn made the current balance deteriorate even more.

The crisis had its centre in Latin America. Unlike some other countries, especially in the Far East (as well as in Europe), which reacted to the oil crisis by tightening their belts, the Latin American governments did not cut back on consumption, but instead borrowed to keep going at the old rate: the external debt of the government sector in all Latin American countries together rose tenfold between 1973 and 1983, while that of their private sector rose fourfold. As their own budgets nevertheless went out of control, hyper-inflation followed in several of the larger countries in the region. A massive flight of capital was the consequence: thus Mexican assets held abroad rose from $3 billion in 1973 to $64 billion in 1984, equivalent to the whole of the country's official foreign debt; in Argentina, capital outflow was equal to 60 per cent of the increase in indebtedness in 1979–81, in Venezuela it was equal to more than 100 per cent. There is therefore some truth in the widespread view at the time that the Latin American problem was a liquidity problem as much as one of a fundamental economic imbalance. Basically, the governments in the region as well as their richer citizens had acted with exceptional irresponsibility.

The crisis was triggered by the default of Mexico, up to then considered one of the safest debtor countries: it ran out of foreign currency in August 1982. Other countries followed in rapid succession. Countries in default cannot be treated like individuals who owe money and be sold up, nor is the nineteenth-century method of sending a gunboat feasible today. Yet much of the less cautious lending had been done by private banks, whose share in Latin American indebtedness had risen from 11 per cent in 1965–6 to 56 per cent in 1979–80, not by government agencies, so that the loans could not simply be written off as a gesture of political goodwill. Immediate help was offered by the IMF, but in the longer term the problem was solved by 'rescheduling'. This usually meant a reduction in the interest rates payable and a lengthening of the repayment period, so that the annual burden was lightened; it also commonly involved new lending to get through a critical transition period. In 1982, over twenty countries were renegotiating, and by the end of 1983 seventeen Latin American countries had adjustment agreements with the IMF.

Latin America had accounted for about 40 per cent of the outstanding debt by developing countries. Debtors in other areas had problems, too, resolved by similar means. Overall, the debt crisis was overcome with remarkably little sacrifice by the banks; it was eased in part by the world inflation, which lowered the burden on the debtors, but mainly by imposing hardships on the citizens of the poorer nations.

By the late 1980s, confidence was returning in sufficient strength to lead to a new bout of international lending, followed by more difficulties among debtors. By 1993, with $1.6 trillion (million millions) of loans outstanding to the Third World, arrears of interest and capital repayments had risen to $86 billion, from $44 billion in

1987. This time it was the poorer nations of Africa and South Asia which posed the greatest problems, having the heaviest debt servicing burdens: thus in 1990, 30.9 per cent of Indonesian exports went on servicing the foreign debt, in India it was 26.8 per cent and in Bangladesh, 24.5 per cent. Africa, for its part, owed less than 10 per cent of the total debt in 1993, but accounted for 40 per cent of the unpaid arrears. Yet Latin America was not to be forgotten: in 1995 the world had to deal with another Mexican debt crisis.

Once again help was needed for rescheduling. A 'London Club' for commercial banks was paralleled by the IDA Special Debt Reduction Facility of 1989 and by the 'Paris Club' of richer nations, which arranged sixty-four schemes between 1990 and 1993, to carry it out.

MEASURES TO LIBERALIZE TRADE

The post-war settlement also included a drive to reduce direct obstacles to trade on a global basis: trade liberalization was a particular aim of the USA. In 1947, twenty-three nations concluded the General Agreement on Tariffs and Trade (GATT), which took the form of simultaneous tariff concessions by all the contracting parties. The two principles being non-discrimination and reciprocity, it meant that any reduction granted to one trading partner was automatically applied to all others. At the outset numerous tariffs were found to be in existence of little protective value, and there could therefore be, in its first years, a great clearing out leading to a substantial overall reduction in protective tariffs among the members of GATT.

By the time of the meetings held in Geneva in 1961–2 known as the 'Dillon Round', when many more countries had joined, there was a good deal less room to manoeuvre, and little was achieved. The 'Kennedy Round', held in 1963–7, started with the advantage of a more liberal attitude on the part of the American Congress. GATT then proceeded by across-the-board tariff cuts, rather than agreements on individual commodities as had been the practice up to then. The cuts, however, were mostly on manufactures, which led to complaints by the developing countries that their interests had been neglected. GATT had indeed favoured them by permitting them to gain preferences without reciprocating, but they had few manufactures to sell.

There followed the 'Tokyo Round' of 1973–9, attended by eighty-three countries plus twenty-five observers. The world depression made progress difficult, but in the end cuts in tariffs of 25–30 per cent were agreed, bringing average rates down from 7 per cent to 5 per cent over the next eight years. Various measures to remove other obstacles were also agreed to, including rules on licensing, on government procurement, on subsidies and arbitrary valuations. Third World countries were to receive more flexible privileges, and measures for health, safety and protection of the environment were debated. But meanwhile, while tariffs on industrial goods were down, protection for agriculture by various clandestine means was rising in the industrialized nations.

These 'unfair' practices, counteracted in part by subsidies and countervailing duties, were included in the topics of the 'Uruguay Round', the toughest to date, attended by 125 countries and running for eight years, from 1986 to 1994. It covered several new areas, including agriculture, textiles and clothing, the particular concern of the developing countries, and intellectual property such as patents and copyright, in which these had been the main 'pirating' culprits. For the first time, a permanent body was set up, the World Trade Organization (WTO), as a vehicle for trade negotiations and surveillance of the existing agreements.

It was calculated at the time that if all the terms of the Uruguay agreement were carried out, it would raise world product by 1 per cent ($212–274 billion, of which the developing countries would get $80 billion) and would increase world trade by 12 per cent. But in the difficult economic conditions of the 1990s, agricultural protection was still rampant, and GATT counted at least 2,000 'contingent protection' measures, such as quotas, anti-dumping duties, voluntary export restraints and the like. However, by comparison with earlier ages, tariff protection for manufactures the world over had become so low as to be almost negligible, and the world owed this to a global approach in which concession by each participant was matched by concessions on the part of all the others. If the surviving non-tariff barriers are to be tackled effectively, it can only be done by a similar transnational approach.

7 Regional policies

THE MARSHALL PLAN

In addition to the global institutions for achieving economic objectives noted in the last chapter, there were also numerous structures and policies designed for similar ends within a more limited regional framework. Western Europe was, together with North America and some other advanced regions, leading in this respect.

An early impetus was provided by the Marshall Plan, named after the American Secretary of State who proposed it in June 1947 in a speech at Harvard University. Its object was to grant temporary aid, out of American resources, to European countries desperately in need of food, fuel, raw materials and capital equipment, but unable to pay for these because of the dollar shortage. Ultimately some $13 billion were made available under the European Recovery Programme (ERP): the largest sums went to Britain ($3,176 million) and France ($2,706 million), and other large grants were made to West Germany, Italy and the Netherlands, smaller grants going to other European countries. The Soviet Union rejected the offer and obliged her eastern European allies to do the same.

It is clear why Europe accepted the aid: the American motives were more difficult to clarify, and they were mixed. In part, no doubt, there was the humanitarian desire to help. The main aim, however, was to consolidate the west against the Soviet Union, and to take the wind out of the sails of socialist and communist parties propagating economic planning and the widening of the welfare state in western Europe. It was also hoped to take surpluses of agricultural produce and steel, among other commodities, off the American market.

Under the plan, it was the European countries themselves which were to devise shopping lists of what they needed most. Different countries had different priorities: thus Britain went for imports which would ease the balance of payments in the short run, while West Germany used the funds for long-term investments. What the Americans, for their part, insisted upon above all was for the Europeans to collaborate and integrate their economies more closely. In the light of later developments, it seems odd that the USA was eager to raise up a major competitor in this way, but at the time, strength against the east was paramount, and European competition appeared chimerical. American pressure did indeed lead to agreements to reduce quantitative trade restrictions within Europe, and to the formation of the Economic Commission for Europe (ECE), as well as of the Organization for European Economic Co-operation (OEEC), later converted to the Organization for Economic Co-operation and Development (OECD).

The OECD remained as a permanent institution, combining the western European countries with those of North America and other industrialized regions – a kind of developed countries' club. It performs significant services in providing economic information and advice, but has not fulfilled early hopes of a more direct influence on events. Apart from this, the overall effects of the Marshall Plan are difficult to evaluate. No doubt it broke some bottlenecks and helped out at some critical points, but claims made at the time that it was responsible to a significant degree for the remarkable economic recovery of Europe after the war would nowadays be widely discounted.

Following the success of the Marshall Plan, Latin America wished to receive similar aid. The Alliance for Progress (which was not unconnected with the Cuban revolution of 1959) was the result, and like the ERP, was linked with demands for structural reform. Between 1961 and 1969, the USA provided $10.3 billion, of which about one-half was in outright grants. The effects were, however, negligible.

THE EUROPEAN ECONOMIC COMMUNITY

In Europe, once the immediate post-war crises were over, the drive for economic co-operation was closely interwoven with the hope of political unity: two devastating wars within one generation had led to the universal wish to prevent a recurrence. The 'arch enemies' Germany and France were at the centre of this drive, but other continental countries were also involved from the start, with Britain and the Scandinavian nations maintaining a benevolent interest.

The first major agreement concerned coal and steel, causes of much friction in the past, especially between France and Germany. Under the Schuman Plan, a European Coal and Steel Community (ECSC) was formed in Paris in 1951 as a permanent organization. Beside the two major partners, Italy, Belgium, the Netherlands and Luxembourg, 'the Six', agreed to abolish all barriers regarding these commodities, making them available on equal terms to all members of the Community. This aim, simple enough on paper, turned out to require an enormous penumbra of ancillary agreements and arrangements, dealing with such matters as transport costs, subsidies, or welfare payments to displaced miners, to name but a few.

Some of these were solved only after lengthy debates and compromises, but the close linkages brought about, and the astonishingly rapid economic growth which occurred at the same time, emboldened the Six to set out a far more ambitious plan of total economic integration of markets, the European Economic Community (EEC), popularly known as the 'Common Market'. The Treaty of Rome, which established it, was signed in 1957, and the EEC came formally into being on the first day of 1958, absorbing the ECSC in due course.

Formally, the EEC was a customs union, providing for completely free trade within its borders and a common tariff against the outside world. But from the beginning it announced more ambitious aims, including ultimate political integration: it was this objective more than any other which persuaded Britain and the Scandinavian countries to refuse the invitation to join. Leaving aside the political aspect, however, the members were also determined from the start to aim for ever closer economic integration and not to consider any earlier stage reached on that road as final. They were also eager to expand the membership as opportunity offered.

The Treaty of Rome envisaged a transitional period when internal tariffs would gradually be reduced in stages to zero. This target was reached ahead of time, in ten-and-a-half years instead of the planned twelve. By 1969, the free movement of labour and capital, as well as commodities, was secured, fiscal divergences were reduced by a single value-added tax (VAT) system, though levied at different rates, and some progress had been made in harmonizing policies on competition as well as on other aspects of the economy.

It should not be assumed that members were simply motivated by an abstract free-trade ideal. Every stage had to be fought over and agreed by mutual concessions involving the particular interests of the various countries and their leading pressure groups. The whole was a patchwork of balanced special interests. Two developments may be cited as examples: the policies regarding agriculture, and the mix of provisions regarding social issues.

It was clear from the start that the free trade on which the Common Market rested would not be applied to farm products: the pressure groups of peasants in such countries as France and Italy, with their large, though declining, and well-organized voting power, were too strong for that. Their protection was to be based on the pre-existing price support systems of member countries, to be replaced by a common consolidated system for most agricultural commodities. Only about one-quarter of the trade was to be simply protected by traditional tariffs.

The original aim of the Common Agricultural Policy (CAP) was to ensure sufficiently high prices for farm products to enable the producers to make a living and encourage them to increase output, thus making the EEC self-sufficient in food. Price targets were set, and they were to be attained mainly by two types of measures: tariffs on imports, the yield to be distributed to benefit home farmers, and an obligation on the EEC itself to buy up any surplus and stockpile or sell it abroad, whenever prices at home dropped below the target levels.

The CAP has been highly controversial from the start. Among the criticisms levied against it was that it caused high prices for consumers and high costs to industry; it damaged the export chances of Third World countries into the rich European market; it encouraged over-production – lately counteracted by subsidies paid for leaving fields barren and for families to leave their farms; it benefited mostly the larger, richer farmers; it opened up possibilities of enormous frauds; and it was extremely expensive. By the mid-1980s it swallowed two-thirds of the whole EEC budget, though determined action reduced this to 51 per cent by 1994. But because of the vested interests involved, basic reform in principle remains unlikely.

In the social sphere, a European Social Fund (ESF) was provided for in the Rome Treaty. Its original purpose was to prepare young people for employment, but its range was widened later. The European Investment Bank (EIB) of 1958 was mainly designed for the less advanced regions and became of great political significance as a form of subsidy for the poorer Mediterranean countries which joined in the 1980s. These aspects were given greater emphasis still by the European Regional Development Fund (ERDF), operative from 1975. By 1994, regional and social expenditure together accounted for 23 per cent of the total Community budget.

The decision making structure of the Community reflects its dual source of power. Governments of the member countries exert their authority through the Council of Ministers, supplemented since 1974 by the 'European Council', a regular meeting of heads of government. The Community for its part is governed by Commissioners, appointed by the member countries but enjoined to ignore their original allegiance and represent community interests alone: with their large civil sevice, they have become a significant independent centre of power of their own. A European Parliament, the forerunners of which went back to 1962, has been directly elected by the people of each country since 1979, and has lately gained more influence with reserve powers over the budget and even over the appointment of Commissioners. There is also a Court of Justice.

Britain, Denmark and Ireland agreed to join in 1972, Greece entered in 1981 and Spain and Portugal in 1986. To the Twelve were added Sweden, Finland and Austria in 1995, making fifteen members in all. Special trading privileges have been granted to Turkey, Malta and Cyprus, also to EFTA, of which more below, as well as to some countries of eastern Europe between 1992 and 1994. Former colonies were extensively privileged by two Yaoundé conventions of 1964 and 1971: in particular, their tropical produce was to enter duty free. The Lomé conventions of 1975 and 1979 which followed were applied to a total of sixty-eight countries and included some provisions for aid, but they still limited privileged access to those commodities only which did not compete with European products. Financial provision under the so-called STABEX and SYSMIN schemes was designed to help to stabilize some of the primary product prices of these countries. There followed Lomé III (1986) and Lomé IV (1990). The African, Caribbean and Pacific (ACP) nations involved now find that up to 99 per cent of their imports to the Community are duty free.

In recent years, expansion has taken place not only in width but also in depth, with the object of advancing to additional forms of integration within the Community. In 1987 the Single European Act came into force. It created a true single market, operative by the beginning of 1993; it added services as an area in which discrimination in favour of own citizens would no longer be permitted; and it strengthened the political power of the Community as against the member governments and extended its competence to questions of technology, environment, monetary affairs and external policy. The impetus was carried forward by the meeting of the European Council in Maastricht in December 1991: the 'Maastricht Treaty' which resulted, came into force in November 1993. Among other provisions, it reshaped the European Community into the European Union (EU), it provided for a common foreign policy and established a common European citizenship and basic social welfare provisions for all, from which, however, Britain claimed exemption. Most controversial were the decisions on monetary integration, for these appeared to lead ultimately to the transfer of power over economic policy in general from the member countries to the centre.

MONETARY INTEGRATION

To understand the monetary issues fully, we have to retrace our steps to the early post-war years. At the time, regional groupings also emerged in the monetary sphere. European co-operation began in 1950, at the time of the dollar shortage. The European Payments Union (EPU), formed in that year, created a clearing system for European countries which allowed them to expand their trade with each other even if the payments between any two of them did not balance, without endangering their precious dollar reserves. It proved to be highly successful, until the easing of the dollar position and the freeing from most currency restrictions by 1958 made it redundant.

Meanwhile another regional monetary grouping, the Sterling Area, showed signs of outliving its usefulness and was gradually being dissolved. Its origin lay in the historical development of the British empire and of sterling as a major world currency. As late as 1946, about half the world's foreign business was still conducted in sterling, Britain was still a great economic power, and no one could foresee at the time how quickly that power would be lost.

By the later 1940s, the Sterling Area was made up largely of colonies and dominions, apart from Canada, in addition to the United Kingdom, plus a number of Middle Eastern Countries. Its main characteristic was that all members kept their central monetary reserves in London and that they used, and husbanded, a common gold and dollar reserve. Payments to outside countries in dollars could be made only with approval from London, though there were some leaks through Kuwait and Hong Kong, and it was difficult to control the disposal of dollars earned and held outside the Area.

To compensate for these limitations, trade, payments and investment within the Sterling Area were unrestricted. This gave the primary producers in the Commonwealth a highly preferential market in Britain, and gave Britain access to raw materials without recourse to precious foreign exchange. While these were felt to be advantageous at the time, it has been doubted whether both groups of countries benefited in the long run from having protected markets rather than be spurred by tough competition, and whether the artificially favourable conditions did not tempt British capital owners to invest too much in the rest of the Sterling Area and too little in modernizing British productive industry.

These misgivings were based to no small extent on the fact that British economic power was waning, and sterling had become a weak currency, as proved by the forced devaluation of the pound by over 30 per cent in 1949. In addition to its external weakness, London's reserve was also endangered by the large 'sterling balances' from within. These were the holdings of other member countries which they had the power to withdraw at any time, as long as the funds stayed within the Sterling Area, and which exceeded London's reserves by a factor of three. Essentially, the question turned on the payments balance of each member. Britain's was weak, and ran a huge deficit with the dollar area; most others also had dollar deficits; only Malaya (as it then was) earned large dollar surpluses for the Sterling Area's central reserve. The free convertibility of sterling in 1958 brought the system effectively to an end. Britain found her trade increasingly directed to Europe, while the oil producers of the Middle East changed to a dollar standard in due course.

The US dollar itself, as noted several times in earlier chapters, did not keep its overwhelming predominance for very long. Though it was used as a reserve currency by the rest of the world and as the key currency within the IMF, the fact that the USA began to run increasing payments deficits was bound to affect the international valuation of the dollar. These deficits had risen from an annual $3 billion in 1967 to $20 billion in 1971, by which time the USA had outstanding dollar liabilities of $68 billion backed by gold and currency reserves of a mere $14 billion.

The Bretton Woods agreements, it will be remembered, were supposed to keep fixed exchange rates between currencies, except when dire necessity forced agreed changes, but such changes were by then occurring with increasing frequency. Thus the pound was devalued once more in 1967, while in 1970–1 the Deutschmark (DM), the French franc, the Netherlands guilder and the Canadian dollar all 'floated' upwards against the dollar, in the face of a desperate attempt by the EEC to keep its central banks in step with each other. Because of the international arrangements, the dollar was overvalued in terms of its real purchasing power, to the disadvantage of American exporters and all those in the USA having to contend with the competition of imports. In a dramatic move, the dollar was devalued in the summer of 1971 by coming off its former parity of $35 to the ounce of gold, and a 10 per cent tariff surcharge on imports was imposed by the USA. It was a turning point in the monetary history of the world.

The 'Group of Ten' major economies who were by then in the habit of taking the lead in these matters met in Washington in December of that year and hammered out the 'Smithsonian Agreement', a form of damage limitation while setting the scene for future monetary arrangements. The dollar–gold ratio was altered to $38 per ounce, though its free convertibility into gold was ended in any case, and the 10 per cent surcharge was taken off again. The other major currencies were revalued against the dollar, and linked to it by an agreement not to let them fluctuate by more than 2.25 per cent above or below their agreed parity. The move from a gold to a dollar standard was thus complete.

The members of the European Economic Community who had quite independently set in train a drive to integrate their currencies, foreshadowed by the Werner Report of 1970, were not satisfied by the Smithsonian Agreement and decided in the following March to impose a tighter alignment with each other, allowing only one-half of the divergence permitted under the former, 1.125 per cent on each side, before action to rectify the position had to be taken: the 'snake in the tunnel'. In addition to the three new members (Britain, Denmark and Ireland), Norway also joined the 'Six' in this arrangement, known as the European Monetary Union (EMU).

It came under stress almost from the start. The pound had to drop out by June 1972, soon after that the Italian lira did likewise, while the DM and the Dutch and Norwegian currencies were floated up. In March 1973 there was a joint float of the European currencies, but the French franc dropped out early in 1974. Meanwhile the shock of the oil price rise of 1973–4 had to be absorbed. It would lead too far to follow all the entries, exits and changes of the EMU in the next few years in detail: clearly, the system as designed in 1972 was not working.

In 1977 a new initiative was proposed in Europe which led to the inauguration in 1979 of the European Monetary System (EMS). The United Kingdom refused to join, and Italy successfully bargained for the right to a wider margin of divergence, but Austria, Sweden and Norway linked themselves informally. The scheme was designed to stabilize currencies in Europe, to form an island of security within an uncertain world.

A central new feature of the EMS was the creation of a new artificial monetary unit, the European Currency Unit, the acronym of which, 'ECU', corresponded by a happy coincidence to an historical French coin. The Ecu was valued by a basket of European currencies, including the British pound, weighted in proportion to the economic weight of each country. Permitted divergences were now calculated from the Ecu value, which meant that for the larger countries the margin was slightly more generous, since the measuring rod, the Ecu, was pulled up or down itself to some extent by the divergent currency.

On its creation, the Ecu was backed by a reserve of 20 per cent of the gold and 20 per cent of the dollar resources held by the central banks of the members. It was intended as a unit of account in Community transactions, but slid into use remarkably quickly not only in government business, but even in inter-bank trading. The reserve which was set up on its creation could be used to tide individual countries over temporary payments imbalances.

If the contracting partners had hoped that their exchange rates were now more firmly fixed, they were quickly shown to be mistaken. Between 1979 and 1983 there were seven currency realignments, and there was a major change in 1986. Part of the problem was the highly volatile American dollar: whenever the speculators operating in world markets thought that it might lose in value, they fled either to the Japanese yen or the DM, thus upsetting the internal relationships within the EMS.

It was against this rather unsatisfactory background that the drive to closer union within Europe of the late 1980s, sketched above, turned also to seek integration in the monetary sphere. Temporary alignments had all proved unstable. In any case, closer political union required common control over monetary policy. The result was the decision to move towards an Economic *and* Monetary Union (EMU).

The central aim of the EMU was the creation of a single European currency. A definitive timetable was set up: a European Monetary Institute, forerunner of a European Central Bank, was created in 1994, and after some intervening steps, a single currency (named the *Euro* since then) was to be established by an irreversible step on 1 January 1999. However, only countries with a sound economy were to be permitted to join at that stage, the criteria of soundness to include a budget deficit of no more than 3 per cent of GDP, a gross public debt of no more than 60 per cent of GDP, and low inflation and low interest rates (measured in relation to the rest of the EU) as well as a recent record of currency stability. Apart from the doubts about how many members would be able to meet these criteria when the time came, several of them have expressed other misgivings, especially over the loss of their traditional power of reducing unemployment and trade imbalances by devaluation. Time will show whether the original timetable can be adhered to.

In its early days, the European Economic Community enjoyed enormous prestige. This was largely because its formation coincided with a remarkably high rate of growth and social rehabilitation, though since then much doubt has been expressed as to how far the Common Market itself had contributed to these. It certainly increased the share of trade of members of the Community with each other: this rose from 34 per cent in 1958 to 53 per cent in 1980, or from 5 per cent to 13 per cent of GDP, growing further since then in part by the adhesion of new members. Whatever the role of the Market itself, the EU is today the most powerful economic unit in the world, with a population about 100 million larger than and a GNP similar to that of the United States. In 1990–2 it accounted for 44 per cent of the world's imports and 43 per cent of exports, as against 14 and 12 per cent, respectively, for the USA.

OTHER REGIONAL GROUPINGS

A group of seven European countries which were keen to abolish tariffs and other trade restrictions without the additional measures of alignment laid down by the Rome Treaty, came together as the European Free Trade Association (EFTA) in 1960. In addition to Britain, they included Portugal, Norway, Denmark, Sweden, Austria and Switzerland, the last three being prevented from joining the EEC, among other reasons, by the fear that the latter's political ambitions might compromise their own neutrality. This consideration was to fall away with the end of the Cold War. After a transitional period of gradual abolition of tariffs, EFTA furthered an increase in trade among its members, but it was weakened when Britain, Denmark and Ireland joined the EEC in 1972. In 1994, the remaining members, Austria, Finland, Iceland, Liechtenstein, Norway and Sweden joined with the EU to form the European Economic Area (EEA). Of these, Austria, Finland and Sweden concluded their negotiations in 1995 to become full members of the EU.

Eastern Europe's answer to the Marshall plan was to establish the Council for Mutual Economic Assistance (COMECON) in 1949. Though its members had planned economies and a controlled foreign trade, and all were dependent in many respects on the Soviet Union, trade and economic co-operation between them remained fairly limited. There was collaboration in science, in the production of some manufactures, in building gas and oil pipelines and in multilateral clearing. COMECON collapsed with the dissolution of the USSR and the ending of communist rule, and its members have turned to the west for closer economic association.

Numerous other regional economic groupings were established in the period, but most of them had only negligible effects. Among them were the Latin American Free Trade Association (LAFTA) of 1960, to become LAIA, the Latin American Integration Association in 1980; CARICOM, the Caribbean Community and Common Market (1973); the Central American Common Market (CACM) of 1961, revived in 1990; the Central African Customs and Economic Union (UDEAC), in force since 1966; the Treaty for Arab Economic Unity, or Arab Common Market (1964); AFTA of the South East Asian nations (1977), widened in 1989 into APEC, to include other Pacific countries, the USA and Canada; the Andean Group (1968); the Cross-Border Initiative of 1993 (CBI) in East Africa; and the Gulf Co-operative Council (GCC) of 1981. None could approach the EEC in significance for trade or growth.

Possibly among the more promising is MERCOSUR of the four countries of the South American 'cone', Argentina, Paraguay, Uruguay and Brazil, established in 1991 with the objective of completing an internal common market and a common external tariff by 1994. COMESA (Common Market for Eastern and Southern Africa) was formed in 1993 with twenty members, planning to have a common market in place by 2000, with the possibility of taking part in the CBI. Lastly there is NAFTA, the North American Free Trade Agreement of 1992, combining the USA, Canada and Mexico. This one promises to have a quite significant impact. The gradual establishment of free trade in commodities and financial services by NAFTA may well lead in the future to the export of capital into Mexico, and increased exports of labour-intensive products from there.

In view of the progressive lowering of tariffs world-wide under the GATT rules, simple regional customs unions will lose a great deal of their appeal and justification. It is likely that several of these initiatives, which were intended more for political appearance than economic reality, will develop into other forms of collaboration and mutual support in the future.

8 Coping with boom and depression

THE PROSPERITY CYCLE

Modern economies are subject to fluctuations, some of which show regular recurrences to form cycles. In our period the most important sequence was one which covered the whole half-century in a single upswing or boom followed, after a turning point in the mid-1970s, by a downswing or depression. In that cycle a large part of the world economy moved in step, for reasons given in Chapters 3 and 6 above. The major industrial economies set the tone, and the dependent economies followed, but tended to fluctuate with greater amplitude. In particular, the relative slow-down after the 1970s was, as described in Chapter 4, much more pronounced over a large part of the Third World as well as in eastern Europe than it was in the west. Some hint of the differences in the experience of growth between the two periods may be derived from Table 2.1, p. 14, which also shows a rather different rhythm for the whole of the Far East.

Various indicators may be used to distinguish these two phases from each other. The most obvious are the rate of growth, which was faster in the first part, and the rate of unemployment, which was higher in the second. Data relating to growth and unemployment in some of the leading countries are shown in Figures 8.1 and 8.2.

The slowing down of the growth rate affected every major economy. As far as unemployment is concerned, the USA and Canada, it will be noticed, had fairly high rates throughout, while Germany and Italy, among the losers in the war, started badly. Yet the general drift is unmistakable: low rates of unemployment up to the 1970s, a significant rise then and a substantial rise thereafter, particularly in Europe. By any historical standard, unemployment

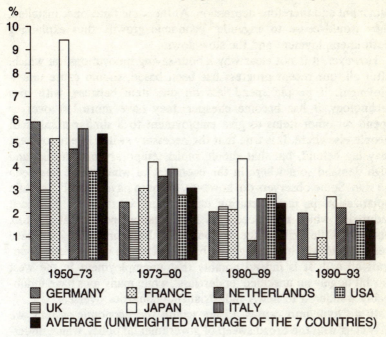

Figure 8.1 Annual growth of GDP, major economies, 1950–1993
Sources: Angus Maddison (1982) *Phases of Capitalist Development*: Oxford and New York; OECD, *Economic Outlook*

in the 'Golden Age' to the early 1970s was quite exceptionally low, but in the 1980s to 1990s had become grievously high.

How is the ending of the 'Golden Age' to be accounted for? There is no generally accepted explanation. Some see it simply as part of one long 'swing' within a series of cycles which began to appear by the early nineteenth century. But this itself is controversial, and merely pushes the question back one stage: what caused these cycles?

One of the current explanations for the sequence of rise and fall traces it to an origin outside the economic sphere: it is technological change which is said to be ultimately responsible for the cycle. Economic swings in the past have indeed been linked by some historians to the appearance of clusters of major innovations, and it seemed reasonable to point to the electronic revolution, and in particular to information and control technology, as a similar trigger in our period. Massed installation of these units, as well as other labour-saving devices, it was thought, would cause widespread unemployment and therefore depression. At the same time, once installed, they would cease to engender economic growth, thus explaining both unemployment and the slow-down.

However, it is not clear why labour-saving innovations, on which, after all, our recent progress has been based, should cause unemployment: if people spend less on one item because, with new technology, it has become cheaper, they have more left over to spend on other items to give employment to a similar number of people elsewhere. It is true that the necessary switch in employment may lag behind, but that should mean temporary bottlenecks and high demand somewhere in the economy, of which there has been no sign. Some observers do, however, claim to have noticed a certain polarization in manufacturing employment in the new high-tech industries, which now need very highly skilled persons at the top, but very little skill at the bottom, and those unskilled jobs have been taken over increasingly by branch factories in low-wage countries abroad. It is indeed notable that unemployment in the west has hit largely an unskilled 'underclass', while many jobs have indubitably wandered to newly industrializing countries overseas.

If we look into causes arising *within* the economic system, we may start with the broad sweep of governmental policy, which underwent a sea change, corresponding to our two phases. To pursue this theme, we have to remind ourselves that economic developments as described here do not proceed in a political vacuum. While setting a kind of technical framework within which governments and other political agents have to operate, they may themselves be affected to a very material extent by political decisions on a national and international basis.

In the present context the years up to the 1970s stood under the influence of Keynesian economic theory, while the 1980s and 1990s were dominated by Monetarism. There were also other systemic changes: thus the first phase saw a tendency to planning and the socialization of industry, as well as an extension of the welfare state, while the second moved in the opposite direction, towards *laissez-faire* and an unfettered market economy; and while the first saw a levelling up of incomes, the second was marked by growing income inequality. The conclusion easily suggests itself that all of these were interconnected, and together may provide a convincing explanation of the observed changes in both growth and employment.

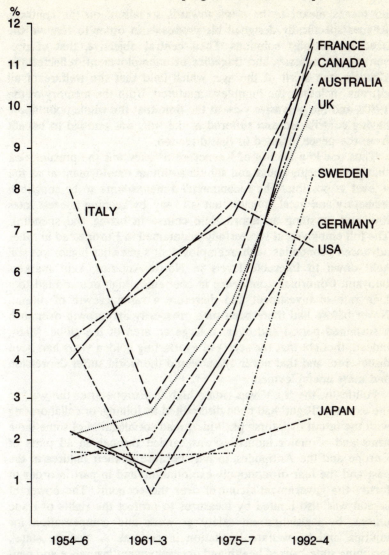

Figure 8.2 Unemployment as a percentage of the labour force, major countries, 1954–1994
Source: OECD, *Main Economic Indicators*

THE BOOM PHASE

Keynesian prescriptions, as they came to dominate, consciously or not, the economic policies of most countries in the west, were by no means meant to be steps towards socialism: on the contrary, Keynes specifically designed his proposals in order to remove the need for socialist solutions. Their central objective, that of preventing the miseries and tragedies of unemployment, reflected the *Zeitgeist*, the spirit of the age, which held that the welfare of all citizens, including the humblest, mattered. Both the memory of the 1930s, and the pervasive view at the time that the whole population, having contributed and suffered in the war, was entitled to benefit from the peace, pointed in that direction.

Thus one key feature of Keynesian policies was the presumption that governments could and should maintain employment at as full a level as possible. The recommended means were to be sought in monetary and fiscal policies, that is to say, by keeping interest rates low, and pursuing an appropriate course in taxing and spending. The full employment successfully maintained in Europe and in other advanced economies, with unemployment somewhat higher yet still held down to tolerable levels in North America, kept markets buoyant. Confirmed confidence in continuing high demand led to a high rate of investment and therefore a rapid growth of output. Never before had there been such prosperity and growth over such a sustained period and over so large an area of the globe. Many, indeed, thought that the secret of everlasting golden years had been discovered, and that never again would the world suffer depression and mass unemployment.

Politically, the 'Left' was riding high in Europe after the war, as the extreme 'Right' had been discredited by joining, or collaborating with the fascist dictatorships. Widespread socialization of some large firms and of major industries was carried through in all parts of Europe and the Antipodes, in part because of their failures in the past and the fear of monopoly exploitation, and in part in order to fortify the government's control over the economy. The power of capital was also limited by measures to protect the rights of trade unions, by legislation on safety at work and compensation for injuries, and by welfare legislation in general. A 'welfare state', including state-backed health and unemployment insurance and pensions for all, became the rule. The expansion of free educational provision at all levels aided social mobility, just as the availability of jobs aided the industrial and geographical mobility of labour. It is not difficult to see why broadly 'Keynesian' policies enjoyed widespread public support.

One key economic feature of the age brought about by full employment was the strong bargaining power of wage and salary earners. Used hesitantly at first, when people in general, remembering the post-war slump of 1920, expected something similar to reappear, that power was used with increasing confidence as full employment looked set to continue. Wages and salaries not only kept pace with the rise in productivity, at times they raced ahead, and as the relative share of wages rose, that of profits declined. The result was a gradual 'profit squeeze': taking the six largest OECD economies together, the share of profits was reduced by an average of:

−1.1 per cent in the early 1960s,
−1.0 per cent in the late 1960s,
−3.9 per cent in the early 1970s and
−24.4 per cent in 1973–5,

the downward trend being reversed only in 1975–9, when the share went up by +6.0 per cent a year. Profit *rates* on capital earned reflected this fall, showing the following averages:

1951–3	16.3 per cent
1961–3	14.8 per cent
1971–3	13.0 per cent
1981–3	9.3 per cent[1]

It had been widely assumed on theoretical grounds that since savings and investment were made mainly by the rich, squeezing profits would reduce investment and therefore slow down growth, but such did not prove to be the case. Investment remained high, to propel the economy forward at a fast rate. Among the reasons for this unexpected boom was not merely, as we have seen, that high demand kept optimism and expectations high; it was also the case that savings to be channelled into investment were being increasingly made by institutional investors, such as insurance societies and pension funds, both of which flourished in this phase, and not simply by rich individuals. These funds, incidentally, now form a very large part of the capital market. Thus pension funds had net assets of £451 billion at the end of 1994, representing 30 per cent of securities traded on the London Stock Exchange; Unit Trusts held £107 billion, Investment Trusts £49 billion and the twelve largest Insurance Companies £407 billion at the end of 1995. Their managers have tended increasingly to wield a major, and at times even a decisive influence on the decision making of large joint-stock companies. Furthermore, as wealth spread downwards, a larger proportion of the more humble classes could also begin to save some of their income.

Rising wages did not merely squeeze profits: they also tended to put pressure on prices. Employers, unwilling to risk losing orders, were prepared to accede to wage demands, hoping to recoup themselves without too much trouble by raising their own prices in a buoyant market. Indeed, the question presents itself why the freedom to raise money wages and costs in a full employment economy did not lead to faster inflation from the start. A major cause was the success of the system itself: the tangible improvement in real incomes and living standards achieved year by year by wage and salary earners could be accommodated by the economy without significant inflationary pressure as long as its real output rose by a similar rate of 4–6 per cent per annum.

The 'Golden Age' of 1950–73 was not entirely without such inflationary pressure, but it was at a low rate and seemed a small price to pay for rising wealth and prosperity. After two decades, towards the end of the 1960s, however, the inflation rate showed signs of creeping up. Possibly trade unions were becoming over-confident; more likely, the high rate of growth was coming to an end as the technological catching-up phase tapered off, so that a gap began to open out gradually between the declining productivity increases and the continued high annual wage increases expected and fought for at the wonted rate.

TURNING POINT AND DEPRESSION

Into this unstable situation burst the shock of the OPEC oil price rise of 1973, to be followed by a second in 1979–80. A cut in output allowed the oil-producing countries to force the price of crude oil up fivefold in dollar terms from an index of 146.3 in 1972 (1970 = 100) to 752.1 in 1974, with another threefold rise to 2,209.9 in 1980 and 2,505.8 in 1981: this meant a seventeenfold increase in nine years. In consequence, $64 billion additional money flowed into the coffers of the oil states in the very first year. While the OECD countries' balance of payments deteriorated by $37 billion, much of the rest of the burden had to be carried by the world's poorest countries. It was these Arab oil funds which largely fed the borrowings and the later debt crises of the Third World described in Chapter 6 above. As far as the industrialized world was concerned, it coped remarkably well with the shocks, by carrying through drastic cuts in its oil consumption and at the same time recycling some of the Arab oil money swilling round by absorbing it in the form of capital imports.

However, this successful adjustment to the oil crisis was not without cost. In the given circumstances, there could not simply be a curb on oil imports alone. Since one symptom of the crisis was a sudden deterioration in the balance of payments of the non-oil producers, there had to be a curb on *all* imports, achieved by traditional restrictive policies, mainly by monetary restrictions, but also by fiscal (taxation) measures. There had, in any case, been a short-term acceleration of inflation, a mini-boom, in 1972. Now the axe fell, and real GDP growth of the leading industrial countries slumped from a rate of 8 per cent in the first half of 1973 to one of 3 per cent in the second half. Unemployment shot up, but the incipient inflation was not held back because it was boosted by the oil price rise itself. The world learned to face a new phenomenon: 'stagflation', the appearance together of *both* stagnation and inflation, which, it was thought, had never been suffered together before.

A further negative factor to emerge at precisely that time was the end of the ability of the United States to feed the world's economic expansion by pumping out her dollars to pay for her unfavourable trade balance. Her deficits began to be absorbed by the vast surpluses earned by Japan and Germany. These tended to cancel out the expansionary effects of the dollar flood, which had up to then been used as a base for enlarging credit and monetary circulation in other countries.

In a remarkable switch of world opinion, one country after another, some openly, some shamefacedly, turned away from employment and growth as their main aims of policy, to make containment of inflation their chief target instead. The adoption of that priority was inevitably linked, whether as cause or as effect, by the adoption of monetarist notions in place of Keynesianism, for monetarists not only made the reduction of inflation their main aim, but also claimed that it was Keynesian policies which had caused the inflationary crisis in the first place.

Rising inflation on a global scale appeared to prove them right. Monetarist theory held that price rises could be modified by an appropriately high rate of unemployment: a high level of employment thus not only ceased to be an end of policy, but on the contrary, unemployment became a weapon in the armoury of monetarist targeting, together with other, purely monetary methods of attempting to hold down price rises. In their extreme form, as practised in the USA and in Britain, these policies came to be known as Reaganomics and Thatcherism, respectively. Their result, as we have seen, was falling employment, slower growth, and a growing section of the population condemned to poverty and idleness.

Looking back over the past twenty years, one may legitimately wonder why anyone should wish the Golden Age to come to an end, and be so eager to reverse a policy which had been successful beyond all expectation for almost a whole generation. At an abstract, theoretical level, there were no doubt those who, with some of the disastrous experiences of hyper-inflation on the European continent in the immediate post-war years and in Latin America in mind, genuinely thought that inflation, if not curbed, would bring to an end any hope of prosperity and social peace.

However, there was, in the advanced world, no sign of such hyper-inflation, and in any case, few politicians are swayed by purely abstract theory or hypothetical dangers. The cause of the reversal of the *Zeitgeist* may safely be sought in more mundane considerations. It is worth remembering in this context that not everyone benefited by the Golden Age. It included, let us recall, the profit squeeze, and with the decline of profit was associated a loss of power over the labour market, and over their own work force, on the part of the owners and controllers of capital.

Just as Keynesianism combined some of the ideals of the Left, monetarism easily became an ideology embraced by the political Right. Apart from restoring the power of capital and management over labour, it had other desirable features from their point of view. Since, according to its teaching, inflation was best curbed by monetary means, and since it is governments which are responsible for creating money inflation by excessive borrowing which itself is due to unbalanced budgets, that is, spending more than they collected in taxes, cuts in government expenditure became a main ingredient of monetarist policy. What better element to cut than social welfare programmes? It was indeed believed that it was generous unemployment benefit which allowed unions to hold up wages despite the army of the unemployed outside in the cold looking for work. The cutting back of out-of-work benefits, together with other welfare payments, would relieve the taxpayer, reduce inflationary pressure, and at the same time turn the labour market more in favour of the employer.

A drive also began in almost every country to reverse the process of nationalization, by privatizing socialized enterprises. Some impetus for this was derived clearly from the somewhat doctrinaire notion, held with various degrees of conviction, that private business was always run more efficiently than enterprises in public ownership.

But it could not be overlooked that their transfer to private owner-ship would also increase the opportunities for making profits.

Cuts in wages, the weakening of unions, cuts in taxes, the widening of the sphere of profit-making: all these together increased once more the share of profits and the incomes of the rich. This second phase of our period was thus accompanied by greater inequality of incomes, leading in some cases to an absolute decline in the standard of living of the poorest, at a time when total national income per head was still going up. There were here traditional differences between countries. Thus, according to the World Bank's *Development Report* for 1994, the share of the top *10* per cent of incomes was 2½–3 times as large as that of the bottom *20* per cent about the year 1980 in the Scandina-vian and Low Countries, the German figure was 3.49 times, the American 5.32 times, with Britain at the top with 6.04 times. Within the wage sector alone, the wage differential between those at the top 10 per cent and bottom 10 per cent of the income distribution, *widened* between 1979 and 1989 by 34 per cent in the United Kingdom and by 16 per cent in the USA. In other countries the shift was smaller, but still in the direction of greater inequality, except for Belgium and the Netherlands, Norway and Germany.

Another measure may be derived from the differential between the average wages of the highest and worst-paid industries in each country. Data for some countries are provided in Table 8.1.

Overall, in the industrialized world, GDP continued to rise, though at a more modest rate than before. Behind that rise, as we have seen in Chapter 2, was a seemingly inexorable technological advance which, even though it originated only in a few main regions, yet benefited all the advanced countries. It failed, however, to perco-late to the poorest countries which, as shown above, actually lost out on average in the 1980s and 1990s.

Worst of all was the fate of the planned economies, the former Soviet Union and her eastern neighbours or 'satellites'. With the political collapse of their erstwhile communist governments, the basis of their economies also came to be overturned. The necessary change might have been carried through in a variety of different ways, aided by the willingness of the advanced market economies to help out with public as well as private funds. The method actually chosen reflected the ascendancy of extreme market-oriented doc-trines in the west. Instead of adapting the functioning, even though creaking, economic control mechanisms which had at least provided full employment, broad welfare provisions and a modicum of pros-perity, it was scrapped virtually overnight together with the

Table 8.1 Ratios of wages in the highest to the lowest paid industrial sectors, 1970–1993

	1970	1979	1985	1993
Canada	2.16	2.16	2.57	3.03
USA	1.79	2.22	2.76	2.82
Japan	2.52	2.49	2.76	3.18
Belgium	2.28	2.42	2.11	2.32
Finland	1.53	1.60	1.62	1.76
Germany (West)	1.62	1.57	1.92	2.02
Netherlands	1.54	1.34	2.04	2.12
Switzerland*	1.28	1.42	1.47	1.51
United Kingdom	1.39	1.43	2.27	2.39
Unweighted Averages	1.79	1.85	2.17	2.39

* Males only
Source: *Yearbook of Labour Statistics*

associated system of subsidies and taxation, in favour of unfettered private, profit-seeking enterprise at all levels. Some western firms did indeed launch their enterprises in eastern Europe, and others also came to pick out the plums, but the bulk of the economic structure, including the linkages between producers, suppliers and customers, was allowed to be scrapped, with nothing comparable put in its place.

The catastrophic drop in output noted in Chapter 4 above, accompanied as it was by massive unemployment, was perhaps to be expected in a transitional period, but even after six years there was, outside the former German Democratic Republic into which western Germany was pouring hundreds of billions of D-Marks, little sign of any permanent recovery. Hungary and the Czech Republic had done best, the Russian Commonwealth of Independent States probably worst. There the inability of the state even to find regular pay for the armed forces may have as yet unforeseen political consequences. It is therefore not entirely surprising that after some years of experimenting with a market economy, ever larger numbers of people in these countries came to use their new-found democratic freedoms to give their votes once more to communists for political office.

It is too early to say whether the present monetarist phase is nearing its end. It is a fairly safe prediction, however, that the conjunction of favourable circumstances which created the Golden Age of 1950–73 is likely to remain a unique and unrepeatable episode in world history.

Glossary

Bretton Woods Location of an international conference held in 1944 to settle some post-war economic issues. See Chapter 6, and also **International Monetary Fund, World Bank**.

Capital May be used in a monetary or a real sense. In the monetary sense, it means a sum held for the purpose of deriving an income, such as profits, interest or dividends from it. In the real sense it means goods not useful to consumers by themselves, but used to produce other goods. Examples would be buildings, machines or commercial vehicles.

Cold War The state of hostility between America and her allies and the Soviet Union and her allies between 1947 and *circa* 1989.

Common Market See **European Community**.

Compound interest Adding the interest of every year to the original sum before the next year's interest is calculated. Thus at 10 per cent compound interest, the return on a sum of 100 would be 10 in the first year, but 11 (110 × 10 per cent) in the second, and so on.

Consortia of banks Collaborative groups of banks for particular purposes, without implying a general or permanent merger.

Countervailing duties Taxes imposed on imports to cancel the advantage of foreign suppliers derived from subsidies received from their own government.

Demographic transition The change-over from a phase of high birth and death rates to one of low birth and death rates. Experienced in the west in the late nineteenth and early twentieth centuries.

Devaluation   An official decision by a country or its Central Bank to value its own currency at a lower rate against other currencies or against gold, usually backed by the rate of exchange given by the Central Bank.

Developing countries   Euphemistic term applied to poor, non-industrialized countries. Sometimes also known as **Third World**, being neither in the capitalist west nor the communist east, or **non-aligned countries**, for the same reason.

Ecu   European Currency Unit, an artificial currency made up of a basket of the currencies of the **European Union**.

European Community (EC)   Name given to the **European Economic Community (EEC)** or **Common Market**, formed in 1957 by six countries (since then grown to fifteen), when their purpose began to transcend purely economic integration. In 1984, when even closer association was intended, renamed **European Union (EU)**. See Chapter 7 for details.

Export-led growth   An economic strategy aiming to achieve growth primarily by increasing the supply of goods and services to foreign markets.

Fordism   A form of industrial mass-production organization, developed by Henry Ford, in which work is split into simple repetitive movements carried out on products brought to the operative on a conveyor belt.

Foreign direct investment   Investment by citizens of one country in companies located elsewhere in such a manner that they can control them. Investment without control, for example in government bonds of another country, is known as **Portfolio investment**.

GATT   General Agreement on Tariffs and Trade. A set of international agreements made in a series of conferences for the purpose of reducing the obstacles to trade on an international basis. See pp. 88–89.

Globalization   The spread of productive companies, banks and finance houses over many countries such that action anywhere in the system will have consequences in other parts of the globe.

Gross Domestic Product (GDP)   Sum of all goods and services produced in a country, usually in the space of one year. If the share of the product used to replace capital over the year is deducted, it becomes **Net Domestic Product (NDP)**. **Gross National Product (GNP)** and **Net National Product (NNP)** have similar meanings, but include the effects of imports and exports. See Chapter 1.

Hyper-inflation Inflation at such high levels that prices rise at an accelerating rate simply because further price and cost rises are expected. Implies loss of control by the monetary authorities.

Infrastructure Public utilities such as roads, canals and railways, telephone, power lines etc.

International Monetary Fund (IMF) set up at **Bretton Woods** for the purpose of achieving international currency stability. For details see Chapter 6.

Keynesian Theory An economic doctrine developed by the British economist John Maynard (Lord) Keynes, which claims to explain prosperity cycles and provides methods for dealing with them, and in particular for maintaining full and stable levels of employment.

Mercantilism An economic doctrine, particularly influential in the seventeenth and eighteenth centuries, which held that the object of economic policy was to achieve a surplus of exports over imports, as well as making a country strong and self-sufficient.

Monetarism An economic doctrine, particularly associated with the American economist Milton Friedman, which holds that stability and growth depend on a stable price level. To achieve this aim, correct economic policy would then consist of controlling the supply of 'money', variously defined.

NDP, NNP See **Gross Domestic Product**.

Non-aligned countries See **Developing countries**.

North–South One way of describing the contrast between the rich, developed 'North' and the poor, under-developed 'South' in the world. See also **Developing countries**.

Portfolio investment Investment, commonly abroad, in shares or bonds without having direct control over the companies or organizations concerned.

Primary industries Agriculture and extractive industries such as mining.

Primary Products   Products of primary industries, such as food or raw materials, that have not been worked up further.

Purchasing power parity   Comparison of the price levels of two or more countries *not* by recalculating prices on the basis of the official exchange rates, but on what each of the monetary units will actually buy.

Reserve currency   Governments and central banks need monetary reserves in other than their own currency as a reserve to make payments abroad. These they prefer to hold in currencies which are most likely to be acceptable abroad and least likely to lose in value. In the immediate post-war years the US dollar was favoured; more recently the yen, the D-Mark and the Swiss franc have also been popular.

'Run'   on a bank. Massive withdrawals of funds from a bank caused by the fear that deposits there might not be safe. Usually results in causing the collapse of the troubled bank.

SDRs   Special Drawing Rights. A form of credit made available by the IMF to member countries. See Chapter 6 for details.

Secondary industries or **sector**   Manufacturing and associated activities.

Socialist countries   Beside the Soviet Union, it was Poland, East Germany (the GDR), Hungary, Czechoslovakia, Romania, Bulgaria, Yugoslavia and Albania in eastern Europe, as well as China and some other non-European countries, including Vietnam and Cuba, which adopted the title. Among their common characteristics were public ownership of the major capital assets, a centrally planned and controlled economy, and the political dictatorship by one Marxist (usually Communist) Party dedicated to the furtherance of 'socialism'.

Terms of trade   The ratio between average export and import prices in a country's trade. Several methods of calculating them are possible: the method noted here is technically termed 'net barter terms of trade'.

Tertiary industries or **sector**   The service trades or industries.

Third World   See **Developing countries**.

World Bank   The International Bank for Reconstruction and Development, set up at **Bretton Woods** for providing long-term capital from a wide variety of sources for development schemes in countries short of capital.

Zeitgeist literally, 'spirit of the age'. Implies common, often unconscious and unquestioned thoughts widely shared by people in many countries in one historical period.

Notes

2 PRODUCTION AND PRODUCTIVITY

1 David Morawetz (1977) *Twenty-five Years of Economic Development 1950–1975*: Baltimore, p. 26; S. Kuznets (1966) *Modern Economic Growth: Rate, Structure and Spread*: New Haven and London, pp. 368–9; W. W. Rostow (1978) *The World Economy, History and Prospect*: Austin, Texas, pp. 56–7.
2 Angus Maddison (1982) *Phases of Capitalist Development*: Oxford and New York, pp. 44, 96; Rostow, op. cit., p. 49.
3 D. Julius (1990) *Global Companies and Public Policy*: London, p. 39.
4 Hartmut Schneider (1984) *Meeting Food Needs in a Context of Change*: Paris, p. 64.
5 D. H. Meadows and D. L. Meadows (1972) *The Limits to Growth*: New York.

3 TRADE AND FINANCE

1 W. W. Rostow (1978) *The World Economy, History and Prospect*: Austin, Texas, p. 67.

4 THE CHANGING GEOGRAPHY OF ECONOMIC ACTIVITY

1 W. W. Rostow (1978) *The World Economy, History and Prospect*: Austin, Texas, pp. 52–3; Stephen A. Marglin and Juliet B. Schor (1990) *The Golden Age of Capitalism: Reinterpreting the Postwar Experience*: Oxford, p. 91.
2 David Morawetz (1977) *Twenty-five years of Economic Development 1950–1975*: Baltimore, p. 13.
3 Raul Prebisch (1971) *Change and Development: Latin America's Great Task*: New York, pp. 253–9; John M. Hunter and James W. Foley (1975) *Economic Problems of Latin America*: Boston, Mass., p. 141.

4 R. A. Batchelor, R. L. Major and A. D. Morgan (1980) *Industrialisation and the Basis for Trade*: Cambridge, p. 33.
5 Morawetz, op. cit., p. 16.

5 STANDARDS OF LIVING

1 The figures that follow, in Figure 5.1 and in the text, are based on data in the World Bank, *World Development Report 1995*.
2 Angus Maddison (1982) *Phases of Capitalist Development*: Oxford and New York, pp. 207–8.
3 David Morawetz (1977) *Twenty-five Years of Economic Development 1950–1975*: Baltimore, pp. 34–5.
4 Bread for One World Institute (1992) *Hunger 1993: Uprooted People*: Washington, DC, p. 9.
5 Paul Harrison (1987) *Inside the Third World: the Anatomy of Poverty*: Harmondsworth, p. 258.
6 William Nordhaus and James Tobin (1972) 'Is growth obsolete?', in National Bureau of Economic Research, *Economic Growth*, pp. 1–80.

6 GLOBAL ECONOMIC POLICIES

1 Trade, measured in dollars, had meanwhile increased fiftyfold: Jacob A. Frenkel and Morris Goldstein (eds) (1991) *International Financial Policy*: Washington, DC, p. 132.
2 Edward Clay and John Shaw (eds) (1987) *Poverty, Development and Food*: London, p. 213.

8 COPING WITH BOOM AND DEPRESSION

1 Stephen A. Marglin and Juliet B. Schor (1990) *The Golden Age of Capitalism: Reinterpreting the Postwar Experience*: Oxford, pp. 78, 178.

Further Reading

(Place of publication is London, unless otherwise specified)

GENERAL WORKS

Aldcroft, Derek H. (1978) *The European Economy, 1914–1970*. An introductory text.

Ashworth, W. (1987) *A Short History of the International Economy since 1850*. The last part contains a good introductory account of international organizations and the financial system.

Foreman-Peck, James (1983) *A History of the World Economy. International Economic Relations since 1850*: Brighton. Includes a highly intelligent account of the post-war period; some knowledge of economic terms required.

Kenwood, A. G. and Lougheed, A. L. (1971) *The Growth of the International Economy 1820–1960*. The last part provides an excellent introduction to the period.

Kravis, Irving B., Heston, Alan and Summers, Robert (1978) *International Comparison of Real Product and Purchasing Power*: Baltimore. Intelligent approach to the questions raised by international GNP comparisons.

Kuznets, S. (1966) *Modern Economic Growth: Rate, Structure and Spread*: New Haven and London. The classic first attempt to trace and compare economic growth over longer periods and many countries and establish a pattern. Still well worth reading.

van der Wee, Herman (1986) *Prosperity and Upheaval: the World Economy 1945–1980*: Harmondsworth. Comprehensive, and much the best overall account of its topic in print. To be thoroughly recommended.

REGIONAL STUDIES

Aldcroft, Derek H. and Morewood, Steven (1995) *Economic Change in Eastern Europe since 1918*: Aldershot. A reliable brief textbook.

Berend, Ivan T. (ed.) (1994) *Transition to a Market Economy at the End of the Twentieth Century*: Munich. A collection of well-informed essays by experts on individual central and eastern European countries, with an overview by the editor.

Furtado, Celso (1970) *Economic Development of Latin America*: Cambridge. Classic account of the background to the post-war problems.

Harrison, Paul (1987) *Inside the Third World: the Anatomy of Poverty*: Harmondsworth. An excellent introductory account.

Hunter, John M. and Foley, James W. (1975) *Economic Problems of Latin America*: Boston, Mass. A standard introduction.

Prebisch, Raul (1971) *Change and Development: Latin America's Great Task*: New York. Thoughtful, but controversial comments by Latin America's leading development economist.

Skidmore, T. E. and Smith, P. H. (1992) *Modern Latin America*. A standard text.

Swift, Jeannine (1978) *Economic Development in Latin America*: New York. Political, social and economic weaknesses in relation to growth.

Tussie, Diana (ed.) (1983) *Latin America in the World Economy: New Perspectives*: Aldershot. The interconnections between developments in the rest of the world and the problems of economic growth in Latin America.

COMMERCE AND INDUSTRIES

Batchelor, R. A., Major, R. L. and Morgan, A. D. (1980) *Industrialisation and the Basis for Trade*: Cambridge. A partly theoretical account.

Bloomfield, Gerald (1978) *The World Automotive Industry*: Newton Abbot. A good example of an industrial history on a global scale.

Chenery, Hollis, Robinson, Sherman and Syrquin, Moshe (1986) *Industrialisation and Growth: A Comparative Study*: Oxford. Partly theoretical analysis, based on the experience of a large number of countries. Not for beginners.

Howells, Jeremy and Wood, Michelle (1993) *The Globalisation of Production and Technology*. Particularly useful on research and development in modern high-tech industries.

MONEY AND FINANCE

Frenkel, Jacob A. and Goldstein, Morris (eds) (1991) *International Financial Policy*: Washington, DC. Illuminating detailed essays on the work and role of the International Monetary Fund.

Helleiner, Eric (1994) *States and the Re-emergence of Global Finance: from Bretton Woods to the 1990s*: Ithaca. A reliable account: needs some knowledge of economic terms.

Tew, J. H. B. (1985) *The Evolution of the International Monetary System 1945–85*. A lucid introduction to a complex story.

Versluysen, Eugène L. (1981) *The Political Economy of International Finance*: Farnborough. The best introduction to the complexities of international banking and the euro-currency.

TRANSNATIONAL COMPANIES

Amin, Ash and Thrift, Nigel (eds) (1994) *Globalization, Institutions, and Regional Development in Europe*. Geographers' views on transnational companies and also on Fordism and post-Fordism.

Dunning, J. H. (1993) *The Globalization of Business*. A comprehensive account by a leading expert.

Jones, Geoffrey (1996) *The Evolution of International Business: an Introduction*: London and New York. A clear introductory text for a complex story, especially for regions outside Europe.

Julius, D. (1990) *Global Companies and Public Policy*. A summary and discussion of the debate on the activity of multinationals.

Wood, Neil and Young, Stephen (1979) *The Economics of Multinational Enterprise*. One of the best in a large literature.

CYCLES AND GROWTH

Maddison, Angus (1982) *Phases of Capitalist Development*: Oxford and New York. One of the most important collections of historical statistics on incomes, employment, capital investment, etc., of sixteen leading nations, together with an attempt to see growth in perspective.

Maier, Charles S. (1987) *In Search of Stability: Explorations in Historical Political Economy*: New York. The best attempt to date to analyse the links between political decisions and economic reality in our period.

Marglin, Stephen A. and Schor, Juliet B. (1990) *The Golden Age of Capitalism: Reinterpreting the Postwar Experience*: Oxford. Stimulating, controversial discussion of the dynamic of the world economy in the three decades after World War II.

Milward, A. S. (1984) *The Reconstruction of Western Europe 1945–51*. Much the best account of the processes of economic recovery in Europe after World War II.

Tylecote, Andrew (1993) *The Long Wave in the World Economy: the Current Crisis in Historical Perspective*. An up-to-date version of the long wave, offering a technological explanation.

WORLD HUNGER AND SOCIAL PROBLEMS

Bread for One World Institute (1992) *Hunger 1993: Uprooted People*: Washington, DC. Wide-ranging, well illustrated with graphics and pictures.

Brown, Lester R. (ed.) (1995) *State of the World 1995*. Up-to-date account of environmental damage and remedies.

Clay, Edward and Shaw, John (eds) (1987) *Poverty, Development and Food*. Emphasis on the problems of some of the poorest countries in the world.

McNamara, Robert S. (1985) *Famine. A Man-Made Disaster*: New York. An important book by a leading American and international statesman.

Meadows, D. H. and Meadows, D. L. (1972) *The Limits to Growth*: New York. The classic first major work to draw attention to the damage done to, and the limits imposed by, the environment on continuing economic growth.

Murdoch, William W. (1980) *The Poverty of Nations*: Baltimore. Economic problems of the less developed world.

Nordhaus, William and Tobin, James (1972) 'Is growth obsolete?', in National Bureau of Economic Research, *Economic Growth*, pp. 1–80. A classic discussion.

Schneider, Hartmut (1984) *Meeting Food Needs in a Context of Change*: Paris. The threat of famine and overloading of the environment examined.

World Resources Institute (1993) *World Resources 1992–3*: New York. A reliable work of reference.

DEVELOPING COUNTRIES

Helleiner, G. K. (1990) *The New Global Economy and the Developing Countries*: Aldershot. A clear introduction to problems that have recently arisen for the less developed world.

Morawetz, David (1977) *Twenty-five Years of Economic Development 1950–1975*: Baltimore. Semi-official history of the World Bank, together with an excellent summary of economic data relating to the developing world in that period.

Rostow, W. W. (1978) *The World Economy, History and Prospect*: Austin, Texas. A large tome containing a wealth of information on numerous countries, based on the assumption that all countries must pass through similar stages of industrialization and development.

—— (1980) *Why the Poor Get Richer and the Rich Slow Down*: Austin, Texas. General view of the technical and social catching-up process.

In addition, the annual reports, reviews and statistics of the United Nations and its agencies, of the World Bank and the IMF, of OECD and of the EU will be found invaluable, particularly for their statistical information.

Index